D1502513

THE GOOD FARE AND CHEER OF OLD ENGLAND

Old Inn, Wigmore, Herefordshire

The Good Fare
and Cheer
of Old England

JOAN PARRY DUTTON

Illustrated by J. S. Goodall

REYNAL & COMPANY

NEW YORK

TO
MY MOTHER

Contents

Equivalent Measures

	American	English
1 cup of bread crumbs (fresh)	1½ ounces	3 ounces
1 cup of flour or other powdered grains	4 ounces	5 ounces
1 cup of sugar	7 ounces	8 ounces
1 cup of icing sugar	4½ ounces	5 ounces
1 cup of butter or other fats	8 ounces	8 ounces
1 cup of raisins, etc.	5 ounces	6 ounces
1 cup of grated cheese	4 ounces	4 ounces
1 cup of syrup, etc.	12 ounces	14 ounces

1 English pint	20 fluid ounces
1 American pint	16 fluid ounces
1 American cup	8 fluid ounces
8 American tablespoons	4 fluid ounces
1 American tablespoon	½ fluid ounce
3 American teaspoons	½ fluid ounce
1 English tablespoon	⅔–1 fluid ounce (approx.)
1 English tablespoon	4 teaspoons

Eggs (whole)—1 cup=4–8 eggs
                1 lb. =8–9 eggs

The American measuring tablespoon holds ¼ ounce of flour

THE GOOD FARE AND CHEER OF
OLD ENGLAND

Feathers Inn, Ludlow

1. The Food Back Home

A SOLDIER OVERSEAS, AN EXPATRIATE, the wanderer, remembers in sudden, acutely aware moments the food back home. "I think exultantly and sweetly," a young English soldier wrote in the trenches of France in 1915, "of the one or two or three outstandingly admirable meals of my life. One in Yorkshire, in an inn upon the moors, with a fire of logs and ale and tea and every sort of Yorkshire bakery, especially bears me company."

Once, as a woman "from home," I stood in an Englishman's garden in Texas. The prairie stretched far and wide on every hand, and we talked of England; of the primroses he could not grow in that arid Texas climate, of the Borderland between England and Wales that was our mutual old home-ground. "Oh, do you remember, do you remember Ludlow," he asked, "the Feathers Inn there, and the cold grouse they served for breakfast?"

1

Counterwise, talking of food is an evocative as well as a hungry-making business. There is nothing that makes us reminiscent more quickly than the tasting after a long interval of some favorite childhood drink or dish, unless it is the fragrance of some herb or flower. Even a glass of iced mint tea will do it—"I haven't had that since I was a boy"—and immediately the picture of the old farmhouse, of the kitchen, and the faces around the table comes back as clearly as if it were yesterday.

This book is about the food of my childhood as we had it in season, fresh gathered and harvested from the Herefordshire soil of England that bred us. It is also a story book of some of England's vast array of old-in-origin traditional food.

Americans may sigh a little. Their opinion of British food is pretty bad, and those who start out in Britain for the first time do so with that firmly preconceived idea. Many an American, however, eats at home more British food than he knows, and loves it, as I shall show. Scores of British recipes and the names of their inventors are known over the greater part of the world, but some of this traditional food is only to be found at its best by those who go to its birthplace in search of it. Not quite so famous abroad, these regional dishes are the heirlooms of just one spot on earth, and to an Englishman there born they most poignantly "stand for home."

Old England, and all the things those two words bring to mind, is what most American travelers want to see when they cross the Atlantic, at least for the first time. Old England is a country they already know, in part, since they first learned to read. It is familiar to them with Shakespeare, Charles Dickens, and others of the great as their guides. London, York and Canterbury; thatched cottages and the park-like, pastoral landscape are not strange to them, but rather a series of picture postcards come to life.

The reality of the dream rarely disappoints; the original is better than the reproduction. Even a rainy summer will not mar the overall impression. But the food, almost invariably, sun or rain, is written off as a total loss, as tasteless, monotonous, and generally bad.

Englishmen themselves have lamented the deterioration in their national food, as they lamented their war-time gardens, makeshift and overgrown with weeds. No one needs to be reminded why good food was hard to come by in the forty lean years, say from 1914 to 1954, when it was no time for a traveler to sample or judge the nation's food. The memory of few critics stretches back beyond that time, so that the traveler of today needs to be reminded of the things that English epicures themselves consider good. Before he damns English food wholesale, the traveler should at least know what to ask for, and find out where he is most likely to discover it.

It has been truly said that the history of civilization might be written from the standpoint of food. Traditional English food is every bit as distinctive and varied, county by county, as England's cathedral cities, her country towns and villages, her cottages and gardens, her country houses and her fine old inns. Before the lean years every festival of the calendar, every opening date for fish and game, was celebrated by a feast of the recognized special dish in season. Simplicity was its keynote. The very best materials, and painstaking care in preparing them in the kitchen, characterized English cooking at its best. As such, Englishmen have relished their native food for a thousand years— and still do, as the food-wise may discover.

"Care" was an almost invariable ingredient of the old detailed recipes, and a housewife's care in preparing the traditional dishes ran counterpart to her man's good craftsmanship in the world of industry—a craftsmanship that in the markets of the world caused "Made in England" to be synonymous with "well made." Because Alfred the Great was careless, he is remembered today by the schoolboy not so much as the ninth-century king who finally made a lasting peace with the raiding Danes, but as the king who burnt the cakes. The Great Fire of London in 1666, which started at Pudding Lane and ended at Pie Corner, was caused, so they say, by a boy over-heating an oven. Such historic carelessness may be one of the reasons why Englishmen, unlike Americans, are discouraged from meddling in the kitchen.

In the "good times" of the past England enjoyed a great reputation for food, one that was largely spread first from shire to shire by posting travelers as they went by coach along the dirt-track country roads. A coaching inn was not only a hostelry, a place to spend the night; it was also a farmhouse set beside the road.

An inn-keeper's wife had to store and preserve all kinds of country produce; fish, hams and potted meats, preserves and fillings for hurriedly made tarts and pies. She had to cater for unexpected numbers, for over-long stays on account of snow or floods. She had to improvise and invent dishes that would keep hot, and have on hand a variety of cold standbys. Many of her home-mades such as Harvey sauce and Yorkshire relish are now carried by modern transport over the sea-lanes and the roadways of the entire earth.

The inn also served as a local market where neighboring farmers brought their produce. Travelers who stopped to have their dinner while the horses were being changed or rested would buy Stilton and Cheshire cheeses and Melton Mowbray pies, as townsmen today buy country produce from a road-stand on their way back to town.

Many a small English township would be just another little-known place on the map if food had not made it famous: Stilton in Huntingdonshire; Melton Mowbray in Leicestershire, and Banbury, Oxfordshire, home of the Banbury cake.

It was not long before many a home-made product of farmhouse, inn, and small-town grocer's home, through increasing demand, came to be made on a commercial scale. As the young men of the British Empire scattered themselves over the vast new lands afar they took, or had sent out to them, the prepared foods, the preserved meats, biscuits, jams and marmalade they enjoyed at home. In effect, they became unofficial salesmen of the "Best from Britain" in preserved foods.

Even before all this, however, English cooking was established in many parts of the world. Before the machinery of the Industrial Revolution started the mass production of processed foods, and before food packages marked "Made in England" made such inroads overseas, the young wives of the early colonists had taken with them their mother's or their grandmother's recipes for traditional English food.

Virginia, The Old Dominion, has a great reputation for good food. The first American book on the art of cookery, *The Compleat Housewife, or Accomplish'd Gentlewoman's Companion*, was printed in 1742 by William Parks in Williamsburg, Virginia. In his preface, he frankly admitted that the recipes were but a selection from a much larger book written by a Mrs. E. Smith, and printed earlier in England. Most early Virginia households relied on English cook books or, like Parks' book, on collections of English recipes printed in Virginia.

In the preface to *The Williamsburg Art of Cookery*, published in 1949, Mrs. Helen Bullock informs her readers in turn that the recipes have been chosen from these early American cook books, and from the little handwritten books kept by early housewives and cherished by their descendants, which proved the best source for her material. As you leaf through the pages many a familiar name appears of an old English dish which has long since become an "old Virginia" or "traditional Virginia" recipe: Horseradish sauce, Yorkshire Pudding, Steak and Kidney Pie, Jugged Hare, Pigeon Pie, Welsh Rarebit or "Rabbit," Pickled Walnuts, Tipsy Cake and Trifle, Crumpets and Sally Lunns, the yellow-white buns that Sally "cried" in the streets of fashionable eighteenth-century Bath.

As in Virginia, so over all the English-speaking world, the British have introduced individual dishes of pies and puddings, cakes and biscuits, soups and savouries, condiments and relishes in bewildering assortment. They are famous for the British Breakfast, and the English Tea. And, whereas the French have kept alive their proud cuisine by exporting their chefs, the British have exported their recipes and their food.

"This old recipe cannot be improved upon," is an old-time

Sally Lunn

tag that should be attached to many a dish of old English origin that is easy to make but contains that essential ingredient "care." Yorkshire Pudding is a good example of a perfection of simplicity; likewise the English Trifle which, though rich in ingredients, is perfectly simple to make. But both need care. If this is skimped the resulting mess is nothing but a blasphemous misrepresentation of traditional English food, and a critic should be sure he knows the substance from the shadow.

There was nothing particularly remarkable in the way the Empire's young men unconsciously introduced British food as they pioneered their way around the world. What is remarkable is that so many lines of prepared English food still hold a monopoly, or still maintain first place, in the world's trade. Certain foods, and they are a surprising number, have been made by the same firms from the same recipes for upwards of a hundred years. English foods cannot be too bad if you can find them at this late day enjoying universal favor and proudly displayed on the shelves of the best provision stores all over the world.

Into this lightly tossed salad of recipes and reminiscences, I have put some of the stories, the facts and hearsay about these widely distributed foods. Like Mr. William Parks of Williamsburg, I have included other people's recipes, standard recipes that are common to the books on old English country food. And like the author of *The Williamsburg Art of Cookery*, I have found my mother's memory and the little handwritten family books my best source of material. They say that when three generations have found a way of their fathers to be good, a tradition is born. The food that I was reared on was our family's traditional food, and most of the recipes in this book are family recipes.

My mother and father were each of very large families who lived, generation by generation, within a few miles of each other. In my father's generation, two of his brothers married two of my mother's sisters, and all three families continued to live on or near the old home acres. The tables of each were maintained with the full abundance and rich characteristics of what came to be known in the family as "The Hyde" cooking, after the name of my mother's old home.

My mother at 92 can still give me an exact recipe from memory—her own handwritten recipe book I have with me, six thousand miles away. When I read her answering letter, giving the ingredients and proportions of some special dish, and the methods of making it step by step, I remember the yearly round, the high days and holidays, and the good food that was a part of the rhythm of our lives.

I was born in what might be called an interlude between two

gastronomical eras: Before and After the Tin Can. Or, to put it less brashly, between the age of candlelight and electricity. My remembrances of "before" assure me that for flavor and variety no cooking was better than that of the English country house at that time. It was a period when that Western edge of England, the land of the Welsh Border, was still rich in legendary lore, still haunted with superstitions, still fay and fairylike.

Every day was an adventure in a world of heroes. Not the movie-star and TV heroes of today, but such exciting characters as the poacher and the gamekeeper, the mole catcher, the lamplighter and the muffin man.

I was born, as a long afterthought to my brothers, in a small country town of half-timbered houses, and five miles from my father's and mother's old homes; too late to know either of my grand-parents, and too late to remember at first hand such festivals as Harvest Home, the Cyder Feast, and the Blessing of the Wheat. But I knew their ritual through my father and mother, as though I had been there. The backdrop of their lives, of the festivities and feasts, was the same; and so were the woods and fields, the barns and cottages, the handrail I slid my hands on when I went to bed. Only the characters and the play were different.

"What you lose on the roundabouts you pick up on the swings." That used to be a well-worn tag of the man who took the pennies for a one-time round on the wooden horses at the annual May Fair. The phrase also sums up the difference between the old and the new ways of cooking. Good country food took a long time to prepare, and today most people are willing to forfeit the flavor and variety it produced if they can save time.

It is idle to pretend that Old England is in every respect still Old England. In the last forty years the whole way of living has changed, and eating habits have changed too. People eat less, and until recently, generations of Englishmen raised in the period of two World Wars have known little of their vast store of good traditional food. Housewives have had to readjust themselves to the fact that hired help will forever be hard to come by; they have had to readapt the patient time-consuming ways of preparing elaborate dishes to shortcut methods. The tin can has abolished a good deal of the old country pickling and preserving for winter; the refrigerator has superseded the old larder with its slate salting slabs and cool stone floors—and thereby, in the opinion of many, robbed much fresh food of its flavor.

Still, in England, traditions live long. The old ways change comparatively slowly, and today the Englishman is once more highly interested in his native food. And there are some, maybe, who like myself appreciate traditional food all the more for knowing something of the fact and fiction of its origin. Like many an old thatched cottage restored, and many a ruined garden trimmed and replanted, the old dishes are being revived. Good traditional English food is staging a great comeback.

If Old England is worth the traveler's going thousands of miles to see; if cathedrals, country towns and cottages make any appeal, then it is also worthwhile to seek out the places where one may enjoy traditional English cooking. Failure to enjoy another country's food is often due, in half measure at least, to wanting to find overseas only what one eats at home in expensive holiday mood. This is a disappointing way to go. It is worthwhile to remember that a nation's traditional food is as expressive of national character as its folklore and customs, its literature and music. And he who maintains a stubborn palate and so insists on remaining ignorant of a nation's food, suffers the same loss as the traveler who shuts his mind to another nation's thinking because he refuses to speak or listen to any language but his own.

There is, of course, no accounting for taste. The English like their food plain, their dishes to taste of what they are and supplemented only by those garnishings that enhance rather than mask the flavor of the dish. But he who takes the time and trouble to search for the English gastronome's choice will indeed be hard to please if he does not discover at least some undreamed-of joys in the good fare and cheer of old England.

Make a good breakfast

2. The British Breakfast

"Make a good breakfast, Sir James; I always say a half-breakfasted man is no good!" Galsworthy's Squire Pendyce voiced a national opinion as he urged his guests to eat well before the day's shoot.*

Squire Pendyce, a Victorian, belonged to an age of success. He was a man of the Industrial Revolution, and lived in a time of vast social and economic change. The face of the land changed, and eating habits changed too.

Only a minority of Victorians were content to breakfast on tea or coffee, and toast, and few stuck to the eighteenth-century breakfast of cold meat, cheese, cider or beer. The great mass of the population agreed with the Squire that only a good-breakfasted man was in shape to face that day's affairs with aplomb. "Good" was an understatement for the gargantuan three- or four-

* John Galsworthy, *The Country House*, Putnam, 1907.

course meal they adopted: porridge, fish, bacon and eggs, and other meat dishes, plus toast and marmalade.

These pillars of the Victorian breakfast are still the old reliables of Britain's breakfast fare, though Squire Pendyce's standard for "good" has been somewhat modified, and nowadays Britishers eat a lighter and simpler meal at a sitting. However, the wide choice remains spread over the week, and no other meal comprises so many dishes that are at once typically British and uniquely British in origin. Americans may shudder at beginning the day with kippers and Finnan Haddie, but when they open it with porridge or oatmeal, and pass on to bacon and eggs, toast and marmalade, they are the beneficiaries of the inventive talents of ancient Britons.

Breakfast in my old home was not quite so over-powering as that served on Squire Pendyce's long sideboard, covered with its white cloth and banked with hot and cold dishes, and crowned with a silver lattice basket of fresh fruit. But by today's standards it was an abundant, straight three-course meal. Porridge was a constant, winter and summer. The main course was either fish or meat. To cap the meal, year in and year out, there was always toast, butter and home-made marmalade. Without marmalade it wasn't breakfast.

For fish there were kippers, bloaters or Finnan Haddie and, in their season, the fresh-water trout and grayling which we caught ourselves. For meat there were many variations on the fried bacon theme: bacon and eggs; bacon with liver or kidneys; bacon and pork sausage; bacon and deviled chicken bones; bacon with fried or grilled tomatoes, often accompanied by fried potatoes or potato cakes. Cold home-cured ham and cold pickled bacon were standbys, and in their season cold pigeon pie and mushrooms fried with bacon.

Oatmeal porridge originated in Scotland and has long been Britain's national cereal, a dish that has gone all over the world as part of the British way of life. Scotsmen like it with salt, but southward people prefer it the sweet way, serving it with cream, with white or dark brown sugar sprinkled over it, or with golden syrup.

Sometimes, when very small, I balked at my porridge. My father would coax me to it, making me feel my little bowl of porridge was especially enviable, with the words of the old English nursery tale of Goldilocks and The Three Bears. By the time we got to the chorus of "Who has eaten my porridge?" I was ready to be tempted with a further bribe of cream into accepting my ancient heritage.

Now porridge, like such other simple things as plain boiled potatoes, can easily be ruined. Five-Minute porridge is the tin-can version of what the Scottish crofter called his "stirabout." So I give the rules for proper porridge making later.

Having finished our porridge we were ready for the real business of breakfast, the fish or the meat course. Fish in general may participate in any meal but herring and haddock are essentially breakfast fish in Britain, eaten only occasionally at other meals, as at late high-tea or a light supper.

The culinary names given to these two salt-water fish can be disguising, unless you know that Finnan Haddie is a smoked haddock, and the bloaters, kippers and red herrings are one with the plain herring but prepared and cured in different ways. The old saying: to drag a red herring across the trail, and so confuse the issue, might well be applied to this naming of the variously cured herring. Perhaps the old saw originated from the Battle of Herrings on a February day in 1429, during the Hundred Years War, when Orleans was besieged by the English. The French tried to intercept a supply of food the English were bringing in. The English repulsed the onset by rolling barrels of herrings in the enemy's path, using them like bowls, and won the day, after which they retrieved the herring of course.

Herring and haddock are always available and so may be found on the English breakfast table in all seasons. The fresh herring may be taken straight, grilled or fried in butter or bacon fat, and served with a garnish of parsley and cut lemon.

A kipper is a split, salted and wood-smoked herring, cooked in a pan of boiling water and served ungarnished, rich in its own juice, with the tang of the sea and the aroma of wood smoke about it. A bloater is a herring caught near enough to the coast to bring to port to cure while still fresh—that is, without salt being put upon it in the hood of the drifter. Bloaters are good when grilled, better when properly fried, but to have a bloater at its best you should have a Yarmouth bloater in Yarmouth during October and November, since the fish reaching that harbor then are in prime condition.

Just as a Yarmouth bloater, at the right time of year, is better than any other bloater, so smoked haddock, known as Finnan Haddie, is the incomparable way to eat haddock. It is also by far the best fish—some insist the only possible fish—with which to make kedgeree, which is a dish of rice and flaked fish, garnished with crumbled hard-boiled eggs, and parsley or chives.

The Finnan Haddie takes its name from the small fishing village of Findon, some six miles south of Aberdeen, Scotland. As the story goes, a fire once broke out in Findon, and after it at last had died down, "the maister" pulled out of the embers a smoked haddock, smelt it, tasted it, and found it astonishingly good. The news spread, and with it the popularity of the new way to cure haddock. Findon haddock is now known everywhere affectionately as Finnan Haddie because Finnan and Haddie slip more easily on the tongue than Findon and haddock. Though it now is mostly smoked over oak chips, Findon folk smoke it over burning seaweed.

The first meat for breakfast that comes to mind is bacon, with eggs. It may be a Texan-type of British pride to boast that the British "invented" the fried dish of bacon and eggs, as well as the grilled dish of ham and eggs; anyway they are thought of, by non-English-speaking people the world over, as essentially British fare. Of the two, bacon and eggs is the more widely liked, and has a long popularity behind it. The doctor in *Piers Plowman*, that long poem written in Middle English in the second half of the fourteenth century, ate "egges-y-fryed with grece" on "heighe dees." The habit gained ground, and for at least a hundred and fifty years the dish has been the forte of the British breakfast.

Other bacon variations, the hams and the controversial pork sausage, belong to my chapter on The Pig; liver, kidney, and cold pigeon pie to the chapters on meat and game. Nor is there need to comment here on such breakfast accompaniments as fried or grilled tomatoes. But I do give our recipe for the breakfast potato cakes.

Mushrooms for breakfast! As I write those words my Aunt Mary's kitchen at Ladye Grove, just across the fields from Birley, my father's old home in Herefordshire, comes clear as a color slide before my eyes. I imagine a crisp autumn morning, waiting as the clock on the wall ticked slowly but surely toward the nine o'clock breakfast, sniffing the smell of mushrooms and bacon sizzling in the frying pan.

The English field mushroom, or common mushroom, was so called for the commoner's right in feudal times to gather and graze on fields that were common land. Otherwise there is nothing common about it. *Agaricus campestris* is one of the great delicacies of the natural food of the English countryside, and its gathering one of the joys of early autumn days.

The season is variable, between August and November, for the mushrooms appear only when the weather is muggy—the days sultry and the nights rain-swept and warm—mushroom weather, we called it. No other variety of mushroom, and no commercially grown crop, bears any comparison at all to these transient wild things. And though you can buy your field mushrooms at a store or country market, they are far inferior to those that have been' fresh-picked. Besides, in buying your mushrooms you lose the delight of gathering them, which is hardly less than the delight of eating them.

Mushrooming is a country game of chance. The common mushrooms are choosey, and a likely-looking field may prove barren, or some earlier bird may have stolen a march on you. There is a tradition, as I well remember from sleepy-eyed experience, that to get any mushrooms at all you should be up at dawn. This is nonsense.

The best time to gather mushrooms is in the early evening up to twilight, when the dew is on the grass, and the whiteness of a flower or feather, or even a head of thistledown, may trick you on and on across the meadow in the fading light. But oh, to find, to bend down and pick this fragile, beautiful meadow mushroom; to feel its satin-smooth white umbrella top and see the lining, crinkled pink, beneath; to have for a moment the fragrance of damp autumn earth in the hollow of your hand! To come home in the dusk with a basket of mushrooms on your arm!

Many an evening as a girl I sat on the edge of the kitchen table, my tired legs dangling, never too tired to help prepare the mushrooms I had found for the next morning's breakfast. We peeled the skins, removed the stems, and spread them out on a dish. Then we seasoned them with pepper and salt, and set them to stand overnight in the cool larder. Invariably you are advised to grill mushrooms in melted butter, or stew them in milk, but our way was simply to fry them with bacon until they swam in their black fragrant juice. That is the old way; the poacher's, the shepherd's, the gypsy's way—the only way.

After a mushroom breakfast, there was the marmalade, butter and toast. Marmalade is an inseparable part of the ritual of the British breakfast table, and is not ordinarily eaten at any other meal, except for its appearance on occasion as the sauce for a sponge-like suet pudding, called, on the sauce's account, Marmalade Pudding.

Marmalade is an old word. The earliest known reference to it is dated early in the sixteenth century, when the word was used to describe what we moderns call "jam." Even as late as the end of the eighteenth century an instruction for the making of cherry jam directed that the mixture should be boiled "pretty fast 'till it be a marmalade."

"Marmalet" was the old name given to quince jelly, derived from the Spanish "Marmelo" meaning a quince. And quinces reached England, so historians say, about three hundred years before either the bitter or sweet orange. Who first applied the word "marmalade" specifically to a jam of bitter oranges and sugar is a controversial question, one that in England still makes news. Only in 1957 *The Observer* published correspondence that named fresh claimants to the honor. It is known that a conserve of oranges and sugar was made in England in Henry VIII's time, but no one has a stronger claim to be the first to give the word marmalade its present connotation than the eighteenth-century Mrs. Keiller. Her story is the story of the House of Keiller.

On a stormy day, so it goes, toward the close of the eighteenth century, a ship from Spain took refuge in Dundee Harbor, and its cargo was offered for sale on the quayside. Mr. John Keiller, a grocer in Dundee, could not resist the temptation to buy the Seville oranges and sugar being sold off so cheaply, and to his wife's consternation he had them delivered to his house. Now Mrs. Keiller had been taught by her mother to make "Marmalet," the quince jelly. She decided to boil the Seville oranges with the sugar in the same way as the quinces, and so was born what The House of Keiller proudly declares was the first Orange Marmalade.

Mrs. Keiller distributed marmalade from this windfall cargo among her friends. So spontaneously popular was her new preserve that she and her son James tested it out commercially. It was not long before Mr. Keiller could afford to close his grocery business, and the family went in for making marmalade in a big way. In 1797 the House of James Keiller & Son Ltd., of Dundee, was founded, and its Orange Marmalade was put up in the distinctive glazed white pot in which it is still distributed worldwide in company with a whole range of British rivals.

Oddly enough, the word "marmalade" shows signs of staging a limited come-back to its older, wider association with jam. Marmalades, so called, are now being made from both sweet and bitter oranges, from ginger, tangerines, grapefruit, lemons and limes. Fortnum & Mason's of Piccadilly, for instance, today list 22 kinds of mamalade, including their own "Vintage" varieties matured in cask for five years.

Actually England is and long has been full of Mrs. Keillers, though few have won such fame commercially or developed marmalades quite so distinctive. At my own home, as in many British homes still today, we never thought to buy marmalade any more than we thought to buy mushrooms. Marmalade was always home-made, not because it was cheaper, and certainly not because it was little trouble to make, but because we liked the home kind better and thought the whole messy process well worth the bother. When the bitter or Seville orange came on to the market at the end of January or early in February, we knew it was marmalade-making time. That was that.

Porridge

Allow a handful of oatmeal to a breakfast cupful of water per person. The oatmeal should be trickled into a saucepan of boiling water, and stirred briskly all the while so that the boiling is not diminished.

When the oatmeal is all in, and the porridge boiling steadily, stir vigorously until the porridge thickens. Put on the lid and draw the saucepan to the side, and let it cook thus for about half an hour (the time to serve it is when a wooden spoon will stand upright in the mixture).

A pinch of salt, and this is important, should be added when the porridge has cooked at least 10 minutes, or when it is more than half done. Otherwise salt tends to harden the meal and prevent it swelling. Some porridge makers insist that porridge should be stirred constantly during the cooking, but whichever way you make it, a sharp lookout must be kept for even the smallest lumps, and it should never have a chance to burn. At home we used a double boiler to ensure against this.

Finnan Haddie

Lay the fish, skin side down, on a well-buttered shallow pan. Pour over just enough boiling water and milk, half and half, to cover the fish. Cover the pan tightly, set in a hot oven and cook, according to size, for 20 to 30 minutes.

To serve, slide the fish on to a hot plate, put a good pat of butter on the top, and the lemon-yellow flakes are ready to fall apart.

Finnan Haddie may also be served a la mode, with a poached egg on top and a pat of butter atop the egg.

Potato Cakes

The day previous to using, mash the potatoes with butter. The following morning, shape into flat cakes and dust well with flour. Pop into the frying pan when it is smoking hot and fry to a light brown.

Herrings in Oatmeal

Cut off the heads and tails and fins of fresh herrings, and generally prepare them, splitting them open down the backbone, and taking out as many of the fine bones as possible.

Wipe the fish, salt and pepper it, and dip in the fine oatmeal, pressing it in firmly inside and out. Dot with a very little bacon-fat; grill first one side and then the other for quite ten minutes, so that the oatmeal covering is crisp and bright brown. Serve piping hot, with the drips from the grill and a pat of butter on each.

Herrings are among the most nutritious of all fish; they are also among the cheapest. The fine bones of herrings, as well as other similar salt and fresh-water fish, need not deter you if you do as my father taught me. When these fish are fried or grilled without being first split and the backbone removed, leave the fish on its side on the plate, and run your knife lightly down the center of the side. The meat can then be lifted back from the center outwards, and the backbone is exposed entire, and can be lifted out and put on the side of the plate, leaving the meat almost free of small bones.

English Kedgeree

Boil rice as you would for curry. Remove all skin and bone from a cooked Finnan Haddie, and chop it finely. Cut up the white of a hard-boiled egg. Put two ounces of butter in a pan, and when melted toss in the rice and season with pepper and salt.

Add the fish and the chopped white of egg. Stir in a dessert-spoonful of tomato ketchup or sauce. Toss all together over the fire until it is very hot. Serve with chopped or grated hard-boiled yolk of egg sprinkled over the top.

Marmalade

My mother used a dozen oranges, weighed them, and to every one pound of fruit added three pints of water and one and one-half pounds of sugar.

The oranges were cut in half, the pips taken out, and every ounce of juice squeezed from every half fruit.

The orange halves were then sliced and put into a steen together with the juice, the pips and other odd shreddings from the fruit which were tied up in a muslin bag, and the proper quantity of water, and set to stand until the next day.

This was then boiled until the rinds were tender, the muslin bag with the pips discarded, and all else put back into the steen until the following day. Lastly, the sugar was added and the whole boiled for "all of one and one-half hours," and the year's supply of home marmalade was made.

The muffin man

3. Time For Tea

"IT'S TIME FOR TEA."

Tea time is the Briton's dearest rite. Your true Englishman might be willing to skimp breakfast and settle for a sandwich lunch, but deprive him of tea, and the nation would collapse, its morale irreparably shattered.

Tea time is the most relaxing term in the language to the sons and daughters of John Bull. It signals a pause, a break in work; an excuse to loiter sociably for five or ten minutes, longer if you wish. Generally, the time is four o'clock, or four-thirty, or maybe five in the afternoon; in the northern counties high-tea is around six.

In fact, in England, it is always time for tea. Early morning tea is the cup that cheers in the new day, the starter to the day's business, the prelude to breakfast itself. There is a mid-morning cup for some; an after lunch, after dinner, and a last late nightcap cup for others. But afternoon tea is for all, an institution as strong as the Bank of England.

Tea had been drunk for thousands of years by the Chinese, and a long history was behind it when, in the seventeenth century, it was brought to Europe. An expensive luxury at first, it grew cheaper as trade with the Orient increased; in England tea waxed so popular that the famous coffee houses where the literary great once gathered to talk over their cups of chocolate, cocoa and coffee, went out of business. Before tea parties settled into do-

23

mesticity, however, there was that notorious Tea Party in Boston which helped brew the American Revolutionary War. The English lost their American colonies but held on to their tea.

Most British schoolchildren of today know the rhyme,

> *They threw the tea*
> *Into the sea*
> *Seventeen hundred*
> *And seventy-three.*

But few know that the merchant firm who shipped that cargo to Boston is still trading in tea.

On a modest side street in the City of London you may find the offices of Messrs. Davison, Newman & Company. Founded as a grocery business in 1650, they claim to be the oldest firm of tea merchants in the world. In 1657 they sold the first pound of tea to be brewed in Britain. In those days, tea was shipped into England by the British East India Company; their aggressive agents, Davison and Newman, expanded over the next century until they in turn were shipping tea, spices and sugar to many parts of the world. One of their customers was Henry Lloyd of Boston, and one of their ship-owning carriers was the Boston Quaker, Francis Rotch, whose vessels plied between London and Boston.

Among other matters, the American colonists were "hopping mad" that the East India Company, and its London agents, were given a monopoly of the tea trade, which excluded American merchants from the business. The log of the *Dartmouth,* one of Quaker Rotch's vessels, contains this entry for Thursday, December 16, 1773:

> This 24 hours rainy weather; town meeting this day. Between 6 and 7 o'c. this evening came down to the wharf a body of about 1,000 people; among them were a number dressed and whooping like Indians. They came on board the ship, and unlaid the hatches and went down the hold, where was eighty whole and thirty-four half chests of Tea, which they hoisted upon deck, and hove the Tea all overboard.

Today, Albert Skerritt, managing director of Davison, Newman & Co., and a master tea-taster of 50 years' standing, has evolved a new blend of Indian, Darjeeling and Ceylon tea, and christened it "Boston Harbor."

Lipton's, however, is the name that is synonymous with tea throughout the English-speaking world. "Lipton, Purveyors of Fine Teas and Provisions since 1871—Growers & Suppliers of Tea Throughout the World; The Business upon which the Sun never sets." Behind those proud words is another Anglo-American story of fabulous merchandising adventure, a story every bit as romantic as that of the Boston Tea Party.

"Tommy" Lipton, as the English public always affectionately thought of him, was born in poverty and left school when ten years old. He ended his 81 long years as a merchant prince, a multi-millionaire, the friend of kings and of such famous men as Edison, Henry Ford and Mark Twain. As the Tycoon of Tea, England remembers "Tommy" Lipton as the man who made tea really cheap for everybody. In America, where Lipton Tea is probably the best known blend, he rekindled the taste for tea that had gone overboard with the cargo in Boston harbor. America also remembers him as a great sportsman and a sporting loser, sending his magnificent yachts Shamrock I, II, III, IV and V to compete year after year in the America's Cup races for the Blue Riband of yachting that he never won.

Between the time "Tommy" Lipton left school, and at the age of 21, opened his first Lipton's Market in a Glasgow side street (on a capital of one hundred pounds) he had sailed steerage to New York City and served an apprenticeship in American marketing methods. He sold newspapers in New York, then worked successively on a tobacco and a rice plantation in Virginia and South Carolina, until his health could no longer stand up to the mosquito-ridden heat. When 18, he returned to New York to work in a well-managed provision shop. What he learned there of American salesmanship and advertising he later applied to all his own merchandising. The shop that he opened in Glasgow in 1871 he described as "Just a wee lock-up shop," but added: "My whole heart was in it." In 1958, Lipton's chain of grocery stores numbered almost 550.

"Tommy" Lipton's policy was to sell better goods at lower prices than his competitors. To this end he pioneered new methods. He had his own paper-bag factory and his own printing works for producing display cards and posters. He cut out the middlemen, became producer as well as retailer.

It was not for some time, until after his one shop had become a growing chain of stores, that he gave his major attention to tea. He acquired his own tea plantations in Ceylon, opened blending and packing depots in Calcutta and Colombo, coined the now famous Lipton slogan, "Direct from Tea Garden to Tea Pot."

At the century's turn he moved in to London. Lipton tea at a shilling a pound nearly caused an earthquake in the citadel of tea brokerage, London's Mincing Lane. He exploited the idea of selling tea in sealed packets instead of loose tea weighed out pound by pound from the huge old tea chests. He had his tea blended to suit the water of the district in which it was to be sold, and for testing purposes imported barrels of water from overseas.

He had a flair for publicity, and by any standards his advertising was spectacular. The first tea shipments from the Lipton plantations were paraded through the streets by two hundred men dressed in authentic Singhalese costumes, some marching on foot and others riding on horseback. He bought "the largest cheese in the world"—it weighed three tons—and had it drawn through the streets of Glasgow by a circus elephant. He engaged a balloonist to shower towns with prize-winning telegrams to be cashed for goods at Lipton's stores.

By such ways and means "Tommy" Lipton whetted the taste for tea. Tea was already a popular drink when his tea made its bow, but the price was high; it was not until 1890, when he halved the price per pound, that tea sales really boomed. Lipton's teas are sold now in almost every country of the world.

My mother maintained for years that I could not make what she called a "good cup of tea." I remember once the retort given her by a woman who was serving the tea in a railway restaurant. We had gone in for a cup of tea while waiting for a connecting train. "Are you sure it is a good cup of tea?" my mother asked. "I wouldn't tell you if it wasn't," was the answer she got, and I looked in dumb but gleeful admiration at the woman as though she were my secret ally.

For good tea, there are several "musts." The teapot—a china one is better than the more elegant silver—must be warmed with hot water, then emptied again before the tea is put in; a teaspoonful per person and, for good measure, one for the pot. The water must be boiled in a kettle, not in a pan, and poured onto the tea as soon as the water comes to a lively boil. The tea must then stand for two minutes, must be stirred, and left to stand again for another three minutes before it is fit to pour.

China teas are not as widely popular in England as the India teas. The Chinese blends are less stimulating, perhaps, but they do have a more delicate flavor. One of the most famous, the Earl Grey Mixture, was a blend of scented China tea originated by George Charlton, a London grocer in Charing Cross Road, for the Earl Grey in 1830. On Charlton's death, Jackson's of Piccadilly bought the recipe but forgot to register the name. Although Jackson's is the original Earl Grey Mixture, the blend has been widely copied.

An amusing story is told of Jackson's who, doubtless, firmly resolved never to forget again to register every detail of their trade. One day an old gentleman came in. He said he lived in Ireland and that he wanted them to send him each month two pounds of tea, all in different varieties of one-quarter pound each, and he paid for a year's supply in advance. He never wrote to Jackson's who, faithfully complying with the order, presumed the tiresome niggling was properly received. But one day one of Jackson's clerks who was making up the order said "Oh, hell. No one can possibly really want these tiny quantities of different kinds of tea. I'm just going to send four half-pounds." The general manager overheard. "Oh no, you're not. He paid for the different kinds and that's what he's going to get no matter how tiresome it is."

A year after the first order was placed the old gentleman came in again. It turned out that he had a nephew in some far corner of the Empire, and he wanted to send him a vast parcel each month made up of expensive things. "I just wanted to be quite sure that you would always follow instructions and always send the exact value ordered," he said, "so I thought I would test you with that complicated tea order. If you could keep that up for a year I would know you're the store for me."

China tea weighs lighter than Indian, and more of it should be used in bulk for superior results. Also it is essential that the water should be poured over the tea the precise moment it comes to the boil, and China tea should stand a trifle longer than Indian tea before being poured.

This stop-watch exactitude for India and China teas is, of course, a fine routine of habit in England, and half a minute more or less would be hard to detect. But one thing is certain: my mother, in company with all drinkers of *good* tea in England, would regard the tea-bag simply as a heresy—despite Lipton's.

In 1957, The London *Daily Mail* gave Britain the world's first place as a consumer of tea, at the rate of ten pounds of tea a year for every man, woman and child in the land. Eire stood second, New Zealand third with six and one-quarter lbs. per head, though *The Mail* added, hopefully perhaps, that in the United States the tea habit was increasing, and tea was beginning to challenge coffee. The writer continued:

"Another point about the Americans as tea-drinkers is that they use tea-bags, make their brews by dropping tiny packets of tea, packet and all, into the pot. While purists recoil in horror at this, it does result in less tea being used per brew.

Before the purists become too overwhelmed it should be added that more people in this country are now using tea-bags, for the convenience and economy, and they claim that not one person in a hundred can detect any difference in flavour."

Lipton's have sold their tea in tea-bags in the United States for a long time. And now, once again, they are following the old policy of applying American methods of salesmanship to the English market. They are not only converting more and more of their stores into self-service stores, being among the first in the grocery field to introduce self-service into Britain; they are also extolling the American tea-bag to the British housewife. The *Daily Mail* asked: "Will the tea-bag replace the one-for-each-guest-and-one-for-the-pot tradition?" It is a long guess. In another twenty years, maybe less, the sacred English teapot may be another bygone.

"How do you like your tea?" is still a regular question, at least for servers of tea-pot made tea.

"Just as it comes," is an unfussy answer, but it is no answer at all from a person who insists on a *good* cup of tea. Some like it weak and some like it strong; some like it with lemon, with or without sugar, and some like it with the milk—*not* cream—poured in first, and some prefer the milk poured in last. Though I often give an unfussy answer to that traditional tea-time question, I know there is a distinct difference in the taste according to whether the milk is added first or last. I prefer it first.

The English tea-time can be a formal politeness "where small talk dies in agonies." * Ordinarily it is the most social, the most leisured, the easiest form of hospitality. Every preparation but the actual making of the tea can be made beforehand, which permits undivided attention for a guest. Tea-time can be simple or as elaborate as you wish. An elaborate English tea has to be seen to be believed, with its bread and butter, hot breads or scones, hot teacakes, buttered toast, muffins and buns, sandwiches in variety, and an endless array of cakes.

* Percy Bysshe Shelley, *Peter Bell the Third.*

Visitors are apt sometimes to smile a little at the English tea, thinking it one of these extra unnecessary meals, a custom hedged with formality, and rather a waste of time. But they are wrong who think these things.

Tea is not an unnecessary meal. No one will over-persuade you to resist the temptation of a good cake-maker's art, and you can stay firmly, if you wish, by one or two cups of tea, and one small slice of thin bread and butter. Tea-time is at the well-known ebb of the late afternoon, when tea itself is a great reviver and strengthener; the rite staves off the too early cocktail hour. It lengthens, not shortens, the active English day. After tea, people still have go in them: there is still energy and time for much to be done between tea and the—in England—shorter cocktail time that precedes the evening meal. And, if you eat as well as drink at tea-time, you will not gulp down your pre-dinner aperitif so eagerly on an empty stomach, and the chances are that dinner will taste all the better for your caution, and you won't be so inclined to eat an over-heavy meal.

There is a phrase that comes back to me at times to make me homesick: "Do you remember our walks after tea?" After tea was always the best time for a country walk on a summer's day, when work was done and the shadows lengthened across the fields, and the rabbits, before they were gassed as pests, came out to feed along the hedgerows and the edge of the wood. For in summer time, even after dinner, English people like to be out-doors; in the long, late twilight when it stays light, at mid-summer, until half past nine or ten.

Tea is a man's drink just as much as it is a woman's. I recall that the country postmen, when they pedalled their bicycles a good fifteen to twenty miles on their daily country rounds, would count on a mid-morning cup of farmhouse tea just as much as any housemaid would count on her "elevenses."

David Douglas, the Scottish plant collector, remembered best in the name of the Douglas Fir, who traveled thousands of miles on foot throughout the American Northwest and California, relied more on tea to see him through the days than on any other item of his frugal fare. He called tea the "monarch of all food."

Tea-time is no waste, but a leisured, civilized, wise hour that remains as a custom from more spacious days: it is a tradition that is a product of the rule that only the best traditions survive. And, as you may have gathered by now, "The English Tea" is a very elastic term. It ranges all the way from a bite of bread and butter, and a cup of tea, through all the regional specialties in scones, cakes and buns, to the high teas of Yorkshire, which I remember as massive meals with an assortment of ham, game pies, apple pies, parkin and cheese, hot teacakes, jam and honey and black treacle, and lastly tea.

For me, tea-time covered both nursery tea and children's parties. The parties were occasions of unbridled hilarity, sometimes tears; best party-frock affairs, which as often as not meant a dose of physic next day. But the nursery tea is a fine institution. Essentially a family gathering, it has its uses. The children can eat without any over-correction to their heart's content, and the hour after tea provides the best chance of the day for grown-ups to come and play too. Another virtue is that the nursery tea does away with the need of preparing, for the younger children, a regular last meal.

Later I knew and loved the intimate family tea-time; the country teas in summer, winter teas in town. My memory stretches from the white-dress, white-flannels, green grass-court tennis teas, to the elegant elaborations of garden party teas in full panoply.

Even a stranger, with no open sesame to English private houses, can enjoy a cross-section variety of British teas, tea-shop by tea-shop, region by region, beginning in the south with Cornish splits and ending in the north of England with a vast spread Yorkshire tea; then continuing north across the Border to the Edinburgh tea-shops with their specialities of rich plum-filled Dundee cake, and crisp golden-brown shortcake.

When I think of the English tea-time, several distinct pictures of childhood come to mind. On Sundays, in winter time, punctually around half-past two in the afternoon, the muffin man would make his round, balancing a wooden tray covered neatly with a green cloth on his head, and ringing his bell to let people know he was coming by. And there was the lamplighter. Though he was silent and I never spoke to him, he was my winter tea-time friend.

My tea is nearly ready and the sun has left the sky;
It's time to take the window to see Leerie going by;
For every night at tea-time and before you take your seat,
With lantern and with ladder he comes posting up the street.

For we are very lucky, with a lamp before the door,
And Leerie stops to light it as he lights so many more;
And O! before you hurry by with ladder and with light,
O Leerie, see a little child and nod to him to-night! *

Leerie always did; a nod and a smile. Then the curtains were drawn, the table set for tea, and a dish of hot, buttered crumpets put down in front of the fire to keep warm. If there is anything more "cosy" and comforting on the short afternoons in the winter cold than to sit by a blazing fire, eat hot buttered toast, muffins or crumpets or pikelets, and drink tea, I do not know what it is.

Muffins, crumpets and pikelets are all of the same family, but with marked differences. Muffins must be fresh. They should never be cut, but pulled apart, and the butter must be inserted in thin slices and no attempt made to spread it. Crumpets on the other hand must never be pulled apart. Made in much the same way as muffins, they vary from one locality to another: some are as large as dinner plates; others are small, thick and full of holes, and a pikelet is the north-of-England crumpet of medium size.

Of the three, crumpets are the most popular. I give a recipe, but in today's England, these "curled" or "crimped" crumpet cakes are usually bought ready-cooked from the baker, and toasted on a long fork before a clear fire. When lightly browned the crumpets

* Robert Louis Stevenson, *A Child's Garden of Verses*, 1885.

are lavishly buttered, one by one as they are toasted, and stacked in a covered dish so that the butter soaks down through the soft spongy layers; to keep them hot, they are set on the hearth during tea.

How well I remember the standard, the every-day tea at Birley, my father's old home during the 1920's. Not so much nostalgically because I no longer could do justice to such feasts, but for the sense of the stability and friendliness and well-being that were a part of our country days. We sat around a large table, spread with its white cloth and center bunch of fresh flowers, and crowded with goodies. Whatever the extras, there was always bread and butter, white and brown; there was always honey-in-the-comb as well as jam, and there was always a plum cake which we knew as the Birley cake.

Sandwiches were for summer, delicious extras, and country teas and tennis teas were never complete without them. The first sandwich, incidentally, was not a tea-time extra, but a hearty slice of meat between two pieces of bread served by order of the fourth Earl of Sandwich, who was a tireless gambler and would not allow meals to interfere with the play of either himself or his opponents.

In each of our family homes the tennis teas were almost as monumental as a Yorkshire tea. Apart from the many varieties of cake, and the plates of white, brown and currant bread and butter, there were plates of sandwiches, and their cutting was quite a performance. Although we knew that there was going to be more than enough of good things at tea, we children liked to get a handful of the cut-off and discarded crusts, with a touch of butter and their filling here and there.

In those days it was nothing for the players to cycle six miles or so to a tennis party, and it was always a "must" that there was more than enough to eat at tea. Though the sandwiches were slender and far less substantial than those served up to the Earl of Sandwich, they were usually taken one or two, even three at a time. Of thinly cut bread and butter with the crusts, of course, removed, the small triangular slices were filled with fresh and thinly sliced tomatoes or cucumber, salted and peppered; spread with anchovy or bloater paste, and others stuffed with mustard and cress or water cress.

No ordinary mustard and cress were these. The seeds of the cress were sown in seed boxes in our glass house, and just a week afterward the mustard seeds, a European variety, were similarly planted. Six to eight days later, the tiny, tender shoots of both plantings were ready to cut with scissors. Finely chopped, they made ideal garnishings for hors-d'oeuvres or sandwich fillings. Plates piled high with such sandwiches were on the tea table for the relays of tea, but were also handed around as snacks throughout the long afternoon, together with glasses of home-made lemonade served from big glass water pitchers.

"Water-Cresses! Water-Cresses!" So watercress was cried on spring and summer afternoons in some country towns in watercress growing districts. For tea it is essentially English. We loved to gather it in spring from the water-meadows and have it fresh, at Birley, for tea. We liked it best, not sandwich-wise, but with newly baked brown bread and butter, dipping the bunchy sprays into a little pool of salt on the edge of our plates.

Scones are other English tea-time essentials, and there are scores of slightly varying recipes for these. We had them more in winter, when the fresh salad fillings for sandwiches were not available; hot, split and buttered, or just served whole, for us to spread with either butter or jam, or both.

Among the small cakes we counted three as favorites; rock cakes, almond rocks and cocoanut cakes, which were made from The Hyde recipes. Of the large, slice-cutting cakes, we had seed, sponge and madeira cakes also from The Hyde recipes. Ginger-cake, chocolate and sandwich cakes took their place in turn beside the weekly plum, the cut-and-come-again cake of which we never tired.

A note on sponge cake is in order before giving the teatime recipes. The old English Sponge Cake is made entirely of eggs, sugar and fine flour. The Victorians, by adding butter, produced a different and firmer mixture; the Victorian Sandwich, as this was called, was baked in flat tins, spread with jam and dusted with sugar. Today's cooks are turning the Victorian Sandwich into a layer cake, which is something different again, and miscalling this, according to its filling, "cream sponge," "chocolate sponge," and "sandwich cake."

Crumpets

1 lb. flour
1 yeast cake
1 egg
1 oz. butter
a little salt

> Mix all ingredients together. Beat well and leave to rise until the bubbles form on top.
> Bake on warm gridle or iron plate—or a strong thick frying pan will do with moderate heat underneath.
> Turn when half done.

Scones

1 lb. flour
6 oz. butter
2 oz. lard
baking powder and a pinch of salt
sour milk, or buttermilk, for moistening the dough

> Mix the dough with a knife. Roll out but once if you can. Cut with a cutter to a ¼ inch thickness.
> Bake on a slide near the top of the oven, 15 minutes in a sharp oven.

> Serve whole and warm, to be split at table, and spread with butter and jam.

Rock Cakes

1 lb. flour	2 eggs
½ lb. butter	a pinch of salt and baking powder
½ lb. sugar	a drop or two of lemon flavoring
½ lb. seeded raisins	a little milk to mix

Rub the butter into the flour.
Add the well-beaten eggs and milk
Shape into small cakes and
Bake 15 minutes in the top of a quick oven.

Cocoanut Cakes

6 oz. shredded cocoanut
2 whites of eggs
10 oz. superfine sugar

Beat the whites of eggs to a stiff froth.
Add the other ingredients and form into pyramids.
Place these on paper on a baking slide.
Bake in a cool oven until just colored a very light brown.

Almond Rocks

½ lb. of flour
½ lb. sugar
½ lb. butter
2 eggs
2 oz. almonds
a pinch of baking powder
1 tablespoon of cream or milk

Mix the butter, sugar and flour together, rubbing the butter
   in with the fingers.
Add the beaten eggs and cream or milk.
Knead well and place on a baking sheet, to bake in rock-like
   shapes, placing the almonds on top as decoration.

The Birley Plum Cake

½ lb. flour
6 oz. margarine
6 oz. brown sugar
6 oz. seeded raisins
6 oz. currants
2 eggs
3 tablespoons of milk
1 oz. glace cherries
1 tablespoon vinegar
1 dessert spoon of molasses
a pinch of salt and baking powder

Cream the butter and sugar together.
Add the eggs, one at a time, together with a spoonful of flour.
Beat thoroughly.
Add the vinegar and another tablespoon of flour.
Mix in the molasses and more flour.
Lastly, add the milk, the remaining molasses and flour.
Add the fruit, mixing all well together.
Bake for one hour in a hot oven at first, gradually cooling to
  a moderate oven.

The Hyde Lunch Cake

1 lb. flour
1 lb. brown sugar
½ lb. butter (or half lard and margarine)
½ lb. seeded raisins
2 eggs (beaten and added last)
1 tablespoonful baking powder
1 teaspoon of brandy or sherry was a frequent addition
Add a little milk if required

The tin should be lined inside with greased paper.

Bake for 1 hour in a quick oven at first, cooling gradually to
  a moderate oven: 2 hours in all.

A richer edition of this cake was also made by adding:

¼ lb. extra of seeded raisins (¾ lb. in all)
3 oz. almonds
5 eggs instead of 2
a gill of brandy

This took three hours to bake.

These two, together with Dundee Cake, the recipe for which is given at the end of the next chapter, are to my taste the plums of the Plum Cakes, recipes for which are legion.

Madeira Cake

¼ lb. flour
¼ lb. sugar
¼ lb. butter
2 eggs
1 teaspoon baking powder
a few drops of lemon flavoring

Beat the butter to a cream.
Add the sugar and the eggs, one by one, dropping them into the mixture whole, without breaking.
Beat all together. Add the flavoring.
Bake 1 hour in a moderate oven.

This cake, served with Madeira wine, was the nineteenth-century version of today's light refreshment, sherry and biscuits. I well remember that when, as a teenager, I bicycled some six miles to visit one of my father's sisters, arriving usually about 11 in the morning, I was always given a slice of Madeira Cake and a glass of Madeira wine, and it gave me a very grown-up feeling.

The Old English Sponge Cake

The standard mixture for the old English sponge cake was:
5 eggs
The weight of 4 eggs in sugar
The weight of 3 eggs in flour

The Hyde recipe was:

10 eggs
The weight of 10 eggs in sugar
The weight of 8 eggs in flour
½ lb. ground rice

Beat eggs and sugar for ¼ hour, thoroughly (this was by hand).

Add flour and rice, and lemon flavoring or sherry.

Beat mixture again, thoroughly.

Butter the cake tins, and dredge the sides thickly with sugar and flour.

"Lift in" the sponge mixture.

Bake until the cake is just firm.

Time for tea

Seed Cake

This is an old favorite. Tusser speaks lovingly of it in 1477, but it demands, I think, an acquired taste.

1 lb. margarine
1 lb. sugar
1 lb. flour
4 eggs
2 oz. caraway seeds

Beat the butter to a cream.
Add sugar and beat.
Add the well-beaten eggs, and about 2 tablespoons of mil'
Beat again, and add the caraway seeds at the last.
Line cake tins with greased paper.
Bake in a moderate oven.

Sandwich Cake

The weight of 3 eggs in butter, sugar and flour

Beat the butter and sugar to a cream.
Add the eggs slowly, the yolks and white being first beaten
   separately, the whites to a stiff froth.
Beat well again, and add 1 teaspoonful baking powder.
Divide mixture into two parts.
Bake in a fairly quick oven on round flat sandwich tins.
When baked and cool, spread any jam of your choice on one
   half of the cake. Place the other half on top, and sprinkle
   with superfine sugar.

4. Old-Time Buns and Cakes

THERE IS HARDLY A COUNTY in England that does not possess its own old-time cakes and buns, and bakers who revel in producing them to the local pride and taste. They rank next to bread as a part of a baker's stock-in-trade.

Almost all of these old-timers were first associated with some church feast or country fair, such as the annual commemoration of a church's dedication, followed by a merry-making fair—Revels as they are known in the South, and Wakes in the North. Quite a number of the variable buns and cakes are still made and freely distributed according to the terms of a benefactor's will, or as reminder of some unusual event, like the cakes distributed every Easter Monday in the village of Biddenden in Kent. These are in memory of the Biddenden Maids, Siamese Twins born there in 1100. A device showing the Maids is impressed on the cakes, and it is similar to the sign that stands in the village street.

Such traditionals belong to the days when country people often traveled long distances to a festival, as Chaucer's pilgrims of the *Canterbury Tales* thronged to Canterbury. People favored their local product not simply for its content but its shape and ease in handling, and in time it became an established part of the county life.

A surprising number of such traditionals have survived centuries of change. Some of them are still made only in their old localities, and must be sought out by travelers along the rolling English road. Others like the Bath and Chelsea Buns and the Banbury and Eccles Cakes have become far and wide standard products of the commercial baker's trade; but they are still to be had at their best in the bakeshops of their original home-towns.

The housewives who, as a rule, were the first concocters of the old-time favorites, have remained anonymous in the main. Instead fame has become attached to the name of the master baker or his wife who first popularized, and probably grew rich out of, some specially well-liked regional bit of bakery. Who, by chance, can say whether Johnny Cakes were named for the journeymen who carried such buns in their saddlebags, or whether, in truth, they immortalize the little man of dough, with currants for his eyes and mouth and the buttons on his coat, who slipped off the kitchen table, turned cart-wheels through the open door and down the street, and was seen no more?

An unsolved riddle hovers over the exact origin of almost every traditional item. Leicestershire's Bosworth Humbels are made, so the story goes, from a recipe that was dropped by King Richard III's cook at Bosworth Field, the last battle of the Wars of the Roses where Richard III was killed. History leaves the question open whether the recipe was dropped by accident, or whether the cook hoped to delay the enemy by his tempting bait.

Such questions are endless. Did Catherine of Aragon, the first of Henry VIII's unhappy wives, ever taste the Kattern Cakes of Bedfordshire which are yearly made on St. Catherine's day in memory of the time the queen lived at Ampthill? As for the small

Maids of Honour cakes, some say they date from a day in 1525 when Henry VIII, ever with an eye for the ladies, saw the Maids of Honour for another of his six Queens eating a platter of cakes with such joyous relish that he tried one himself, and found it very good. Another tradition says they were named for Queen Elizabeth's Maids of Honour when she lived at Richmond Palace.

No one knows who first made Cornwall famous for its saffron cakes and buns and Cornish "splits," nor what citizen of Shrews-bury—still pronounced according to the old spelling "Shrowsbury" —first made Shrewsbury Cakes, which have been popular since the reign of Queen Anne. History also is silent about who first baked Rutland's Plum Shuttles, the oval-shaped buns made in the likeness of a weaver's shuttle and flavored with currants and cara-way seeds; sometimes they are also called Valentine Buns because they were carried round on Valentine's Day.

Small cakes and candy—almond comfits, macaroons and candied sticks of angelica—used to be known as "fairings," the presents given or brought from a fair. Gingerbreads, the most widely popu-lar fairings, were associated with fairs long before anyone begged:

> Tom Pearse, Tom Pearse, lend me your grey mare,
> All along, down along, out along, lee.
> For I want to go to Widdecombe Fair.

The popular snack at Widdecombe Fair was spiced ale and gingerbread.

There are probably as many varieties of gingerbread as there are "original recipes." The spicy bread, cake as it used more cor-rectly to be called, was probably made in France and other Euro-pean countries before it became a fifteenth-century English fairing, or before, in London, it became Parliamentary ginger-bread, "Parleys" for short. Hampshire with its gingerbread "hus-bands," Bath with its gingerbread Valentines, and half a dozen other places now vie in tradition with Shropshire's Market Dray-ton as the "original home" of English gingerbread.

In creating this world of gingerbread folk, the plain cake was compounded with molasses and highly flavored with ginger pressed into wooden molds, then baked and gilded. You may still see the early wooden molds for the Bath Valentines displayed in the Bath Pump Room Museum as treasured relics.

Old recipes, like folk tales, have many versions. Taken either from old manuscripts or hand-written notes or time-worn recipe books, these re-copied recipes, like an oft-repeated story, were inevitably changed by the bakers in varying degrees to suit their tastes, particularly in the flavoring ingredients. Housewives, too, "improved" recipes to suit the family taste or pocket. Thus the term original recipe can be a highly debatable one. Enough is it to know that all of the "originals" are at least generations old.

Parkin, the North country oatmeal cakes, one of the homemade traditionals, likewise varies from house to house, and county by county. As recently as August 1958 a request for the Yorkshire Parkin recipe appeared in the London *Daily Telegraph & Morning Post*. Recipes from all over the country swamped the mail, and at least a quarter of the correspondents, indignant and outraged, asserted Lancashire's claim to being the original home of parkin.

Some recipes submitted in the deluge underscored the fact that only oatmeal should be used, never oatmeal and flour. Others prescribed lard or dripping instead of butter. But no one denied that parkin is best kept for a week or two, by which time it will have become "nice and clarty"—soft and sticky: ideal for children to munch in hunks, for picnics and nursery suppers. Parkin or "parkins" is delicious with Cheshire cheese, and is usually displayed in large slabs with a rosy apple on top. In the North of England it is traditionally eaten on November fifth, Bonfire Day or Guy Fawkes' Day, in commemoration of Guy Fawkes' attempt to blow up the Houses of Parliament with gunpowder in 1605. Then, best of all, parkin is enjoyed around a bonfire, with apples, baked potatoes and glasses of hot milk.

The recipe I give for this oatmeal delicacy dates from the reign of George III, and came from the great-great-grandmother of one of the *Daily Telegraph & Morning Post* Lancashire readers. Such a choice is a nice piece of diplomacy, no doubt, but no one in Yorkshire can deny that it produces genuine parkin.

Old as all these traditionals are, they are young in comparison with the Hot Cross Bun. It might be called the mother of all traditional English cakes and buns. Early every Good Friday morning at our house the baker delivered the buns, still warm from his oven, in time for breakfast. It was the only day in the year that they were to be had, not as in America throughout the preceding days of Lent.

I never knew then that I owed that yearly breakfast "special" to my pagan Saxon forebears, that Hot Cross Buns were once among the sacrificial delicacies offered to pagan gods of the ancient world. The Egyptians of old offered cakes imprinted with a pair of horns to their moon goddess. The Greeks offered similar cakes to their divinities, marking them first with a pair of ox horns and later with a cross, perhaps to indicate the four quarters of the moon. The Romans ate cross bread at public sacrifices, buying it at the doors of the temple as they went in. So, too, the pagan Saxons, the Aztecs of Mexico, and the Incas of Peru, had their cross bread.

The early Catholic church adopted cross-marked wafers, and with the rise of Protestantism in England, the cross bun gradually was accepted as the traditional breakfast bun for Good Friday. By 1733 "Hot Cross Buns" had become a street cry in England for every Good Friday morning, and the centerpiece of a folk chant, like the Banbury cakes.

Nobody now "rides a cock-horse to Banbury-cross," but those who visit Banbury in Oxfordshire can still have the true version of the oldest Banbury specialty, Banbury cake. It is a small oval cake of puff paste, enclosing a filling of dried fruit, sweetened with sugar or honey, and flavored with spices, and is the ancestor of the modern mince pie. Renowned for centuries, the ingredients for the cakes were listed as far back as 1586, and there is still an old bake shop in Banbury, built in 1616, which has been filled with the warm fragrance of baking "banburies" ever since it was built. Ben Jonson was particularly partial to "banburies" and praised them in 1604, but it was not until about 1760 that the fame of the Banbury cake became nation-wide.

So with the Eccles cakes, the Banbury counterpart that originated in Eccles, Lancashire, and were associated with the Eccles Wakes. The Eccles bake shop in Church Street is the place to find the cakes at their best. It belonged first to James Birch, a baker who did such a brisk trade in "Eccles" towards the end of the eighteenth century that he moved to larger premises across the street. Subsequently, William Bradburn, one of his former apprentices, reopened the old shop and smartly worded his sign "The Old Original Eccles Cake Shop Never Removed."

Alas, with both "Banburies" and "Eccles" there are, as master bakers unhappily agree, those in the trade who make a true traditional and those who make a bastard cake by an injudicious use of breadcrumbs. So if you want to be sure of a real Banbury and a real Eccles, you should seek each in its own home-town.

The Bath Bun, too, has its variations, and with good reason Fortts' of Bath, famous makers of *the* Bath Oliver Biscuits, pride themselves also on their Original Bath Buns. These, like the biscuits, were products of Bath when the city was as famous for food as New Orleans is today. No one knows who first molded the rich pieces of dough into rounds, and washed them with egg yolks and sprinkled them with caraway comfits. In time the caraway comfits were replaced by a few currants. These, with some coarse sugar nibs sprinkled on the top identify, Bath bakers firmly say, the *real* Bath Bun. Nothing is more infuriating to them than to have London bakers turn out their own version of the Bath masterpieces and then sell the thing as the London Bath Bun. London, they say, has its own specialties—the plain long-fingered London buns with sugar icing, and the richly spiced and sugared Chelsea buns—and London bakers would do better to stick to their own.

London's Chelsea, which is to London what Greenwich Village

is to New York, was famous for its Chelsea buns even before
Bath was a fashionable spa. Among Chelsea's tree-shaded streets,
near the Thames Embankment, you may find the "Kings Arms,"
and see over a fireplace an old business card which bears the
Royal Arms and proclaims that Richard Hand was the "Oldest
Original Chelsey Bunn Baker ... Removed from the Old Original
Chelsey Bunn house."

Four generations of Hands managed the bun business, and for
more than a century and a half the old bake shop situated then in
Jew's Row—now the Pimlico Road near Victoria Station—attracted
crowds of humble and fashionable folk, including both George II
and George III and their queens.

The Hands baked Chelsea buns the year through, but on Good
Friday mornings Hot Cross Buns were also sold. So famous was
the Bun Shop by 1792 that on Good Friday of that year over
fifty thousand Londoners clamored in the street for their Hot
Cross Buns at "a very early hour." The following year Mrs. Hand,
fearing a riot, put up a notice that there would be Chelsea Buns
as usual, but no Hot Cross buns, which is one of the rare instances
in history when too much popularity forced a business to give up
a product. In 1839, when the original bake shop was demolished
and the business transferred to the "Kings Arms," nearly a quarter
of a million Chelsea buns were reported sold.

Which brings me belatedly to shortbread, among the best
known of all Britain's old-time cakes. But for real shortbread you
must go north to Scotland: it is a Scottish pride that traces its
descent directly from the pagan by way of the "Christianized"
Yule-bannock and Scottish Hogmany, or New Year. Like England's gingerbread, Scotland's shortbread was once dignified by
the name of cake, but either as bread or cake it may be relished
any time of the year.

But never is it so prized as at Yuletide. Then the Edinburgh
biscuit makers bake shortbread of many kinds: Yule-brunies that
are round and notched about the rim to symbolize the sun in a
memory survival of sun-worship; others in assorted shapes sug-

gestive of Scottish thistles and tartans; still others elaborately sugar-adorned with such greetings as *A Gude New Year to Ane and A.* And so the Yule-brunies *Frae Bonnie Scotland* travel the world over.

By all means, Scotland's shortbread is included among this chapter's recipes, and for good measure I have noted, too, the recipe for the spiced and fruity plum of baker's plum cakes, Dundee Cake.

Leicestershire Bosworth Jumbels *

8 oz. flour
6 oz. butter
1 lb. sugar
1 large egg

> Beat sugar and butter, and stir in the egg.
> Add flour and mix thoroughly.
> Shape pieces of the mixture into the form of an S and place on a hot greased tin.
> Bake in moderate oven until brown.

Maids of Honour **

Line some patty pans with good puff paste and fill with a mixture of:

½ pint milk
2 tablespoonfuls breadcrumbs
4 oz. butter
2 oz. ground almonds
1 oz. sugar
3 eggs
the grated rind of a lemon

> Boil the milk and crumbs and let them stand for 10 minutes.
> Add the butter, sugar and flavoring.

* Whitbread & Co. Ltd., *Receipts & Relishes.*
** Andre L. Simon, *Guide to Good Food and Wines.*

Beat in the eggs, one at a time.

Put a dessertspoonful of the mixture in the center of the
pastry, and bake a golden brown.

Cornish Splits *

3 lbs. flour

½ lb. butter

2 oz. lard

2 oz. yeast

¼ pint of milk

1 teaspoonful of salt

1 teaspoonful sugar

½ pint warm water

Put yeast in basin with sugar, and add the warm water and
then a tablespoonful of flour.

Cover with a cloth and leave to rise in a warm place.

Put milk, butter and lard in a saucepan to warm.

Warm the flour and put in a mixing bowl.

Make a well in the middle and pour in the milk, etc., and
yeast mixture.

Mix all into a nice soft dough and put to rise as before.

When well risen, knead and place on baking tin in small
rounds and let them rise again.

Bake in a moderate oven.

Take out and rub over, while hot, with a slightly buttered
paper, to give the splits a gloss.

Place them all on a warm blanket or cloth, and cover lightly
with the same. This makes the outside soft instead of crisp.

Approximately 1½ hours is required for the splits to rise
twice.

Serve cold, split open and fill with Cornish cream and jam.

* Florence White, *Good Things in England*, 1932.

Saffron Cake *

1 lb. dough   1 oz. candied peel
½ teaspoon saffron   3 oz. butter
2 oz. castor sugar   3 oz. lard
2 oz. currants

Make the dough in the ordinary way as for bread, but infuse the saffron in the warm water first to make it yellow. When the dough has risen, mix in the currants, sugar and candied peel. Melt together the butter and lard, which must not be made too hot or allowed to oil; pour on to the dough and beat in well. Then knead well; put into a cake-tin and leave to rise to the top of the tin before cooking in a moderate oven.

Shrewsbury Cakes **

Mix well together equal parts of flour, butter and sugar, and the white of one egg per ½ lb. of the other ingredients.

The mixture is then rolled out, cut into rounds, and baked in a quick oven.

Ginger Cake

1 lb. flour
½ lb. butter
½ lb. brown sugar
2 oz. molasses
2 teaspoonfuls ground rice
2 teaspoonfuls bicarbonate soda
2 teaspoonfuls ground ginger
1 egg
1 tablespoonful milk

Place flour in a basin with sieved carbonate of soda, spice and ginger.

* Andre L. Simon, *Guide to Good Food and Wines.*
** Andre L. Simon, *Coming Events in Britain* magazine.

Place butter, sugar and molasses in a saucepan, stir over
fire until melted.

Have ready the well beaten egg, and milk, and stir them into
the flour, spice and ginger.

Add the melted ingredients, butter, sugar and molasses.

When well mixed, spread mixture in a well-greased shallow
tin.

Bake about ½ hour, in a moderate oven.

To prevent burning, place paper over the mixture, and do
not open the oven too soon after putting the mixture to
bake.

Parkin *

½ lb. flour	2 teaspoonfuls ground ginger
¼ lb. oatmeal	a little grated nutmeg
¼ lb. butter or lard	1 teaspoonful mixed spice
¼ lb. brown sugar	½ lb. molasses
pinch of salt	½ teaspoonful bicarbonate of soda
½ cup of warm milk	1 teaspoonful baking powder

Mix together all the dry ingredients except sugar and bicarbonate of soda. Slightly warm the syrup,—molasses, sugar
and fat—and add to the dry ingredients.

Warm the milk. Dissolve soda in it, and add to the mixture.

Stir well to produce a soft consistency. Turn into a well-
greased baking tin.

Bake in a moderate oven for 1-1¼ hours.

Dundee Cake **

½ lb. each of flour, butter, sugar, currants, glace cherries

¼ lb. ground rice

2 oz. mixed spice

3 eggs

2 tablespoons milk

2 tablespoons ground almonds

2 oz. whole almonds

* Mrs. E. Laycock, *The Daily Telegraph & Morning Post.*
** Andre L. Simon, *Guide to Good Food & Wines.*

Beat butter to a cream.

Add sugar, the yolks of egg, one at a time, adding some of the flour between yolks.

Beat egg whites stiff and add them then to the ground rice.

Beat well for 20 minutes.

Add fruit, peel and ground almonds.

Butter cake tins and flour them before putting mixture in.

Cover top of cakes with split almonds before baking.

This mixture makes two cakes.

Shortbread *

10 oz. finest pastry flour

2 oz. rice flour

8 oz. best butter

4 oz. superfine sugar

Dry and sieve the flour and mix with the rice flour.

Squeeze the butter free of moisture.

On a marble slab or baking-board work the butter and sugar together with the hand until thoroughly incorporated; then gradually work in the mixed flours until the dough resembles shortcrust.

Do not roll out, but press with the hand into two round cakes about ¾ inch thick, either in oiled and floured molds, or on a sheet of baking paper.

Notch the edges with finger and thumb, place the cakes in greased sandwich tins or on a baking-sheet, and prick all over with a fork.

Bake at 375 degrees F. for 15 minutes, or until the cakes begin to color. Then reduce to 350 degrees or less, and crisp off slowly for 45-60 minutes.

Remove and leave to become cool and firm in the tin. Then turn out carefully on to a wire tray.

When quite cold, wrap in waxed paper and store in an airtight tin.

* F. Marian McNeill, *Coming Events in Britain* magazine.

The River Lugg

5. Oddsfish!

It DEPENDS, OF COURSE, on your viewpoint. England has been called an island entirely bounded by fish. The Romans' viewpoint was more specific. Those ancient conquerors thought of England as the home of the known world's most delectable oysters, and some surmise that the oyster was the main reason for the Roman conquest of barbaric Britain. During their occupation they thought it worth while to ship Essex and Kentish oysters to Rome, some 900 miles away by slow boat.

The Dutch at one time thought of England in terms of herring. They waged, and lost, a long and bitter struggle for the herring fisheries off the coast. Thus historians claim that the herring helped lay the foundation of British sea power, and that the herring is as much a part of England's history as Nelson and Trafalgar. Right up to the present the humble herring has been no small item of British trade. Before World War I, Britain exported over

53

five million pounds sterling worth of salt herring, and consumed over four million pounds worth at home. Though these figures have decreased, the trade in herrings at home and by sea is still substantial and brisk.

My own view of fish-rich Britain turns inland, and I see two small rivers of Herefordshire, the Arrow and the Lugg—creeks they would be called in America—where I fished with my father.

At first I had to be content with a float and a worm. But I caught my first good-sized trout when I was eight years old, dressed, I remember, in my favorite red coat, for my father held on to me by my coat-tails for fear I would be drawn into the water as I brought the fighting trout in. After that feat I spent hours of practice in casting a fly on the grass tennis lawn, and at last I was allowed to fish with a fly from the river banks.

Many an English angler's afterthoughts have become, like Izaak Walton's *The Compleat Angler*, classics in literature—books which not only describe the art of angling but are packed with sage observations on the whole life of a river. So for me. Along those winding, often willow-bordered rivers I learned "the secret of observation: stillness, silence, and apparent indifference." *
Sometimes even the shy otter would come on us unawares. I would long to pluck my father by the arm and nod to him, so that he might see the otter too. But I knew that I would be in sheer disgrace if I should frighten our visitor away with the slightest movement of head or hand; besides, my father never seemed to miss a thing. So I stood as if turned to stone, inwardly bubbling with excitement while the otter took its place among my most valued friends.

Our little rivers held no salmon, the king of freshwater fish and the epicure's first choice, but we could buy it very fresh from the salmon rivers, the Severn and the Wye. Trout and the beautiful silvered, shimmering grayling were our major goals, though we did not scorn perch, roach, gudgeon, and in winter pike, the shark of the English rivers.

* Richard Jefferies, *The Open Air*, 1885.

Opening dates of fishing seasons were the markers in our country year. June was the high time; when the hedgerows were full of the wild rose and elder blossoms, when the water-meadows were brightest and the river banks thickset with yellow iris and forget-me-not; then the trout were best and strongest. Evening after evening we would go to one of our rivers for the evening rise. The fish were easier to see then in the darkening stream, and they came more readily to the fly.

Never a day was lost that we spent along the rivers. If our catch was good, there was always that triumphant moment at the end of the long walk home, when we took the fish from the grass-lined creel and displayed them on a dish, kneeling in the late dusk on a patch of lawn outside the kitchen door. And if the catch was poor we always had something else to delight us—as with all fishermen, "special days and successes he will no doubt recall, but always with the remembrance and the mind's vision of the scenes and the world in which he fished." *

But all rivers wind to the sea, and most of the fish that come to British tables are the shell and salt-water fish abounding in the seas about Britain's coasts. Of this fishy multitude I have dealt with the important members of the herring family in my discussion of breakfast. Among many others are the richly oiled silver-blue mackerel, the red mullet, and the pilchard and diminutive whitebait, which are the young of herrings and sprats.

Pilchards are really fine fat sardines, the fattest members of the herring family. Too large for canning, they are excellent when plain broiled, but being bad travelers they should be eaten where they are most abundantly caught—along the coastlines of Devon and Cornwall. As for whitebait, it used to be fashionable to go down the River Thames to Greenwich and eat whitebait cooked fresh from the nets. For a hundred years after 1765, Members of Parliament dined off whitebait annually at Greenwich, but this custom has rightly gone by the board. Delectable as whitebait are, they should be eaten not with ceremony but

* Viscount Grey of Fallodon, *Fly Fishing*, 1899.

in private, messy contentment with brown bread and butter, and lemon.

Cod and hake are cousins. Cod, always a great English standby, is the steady Lenten and fasting dish. Hake, a bit superior, has an outstanding virtue: it is almost free of side bones, and its backbone detaches more easily than that of any other fish I know. Surely hake is the safest fish for children and those whose eyesight is not what it once was.

Flat fish are another great family, but one that is undistinguished with the noble exception of the sole. And like so many other species of fish, the European sole is different from the American soles. The gastronomes' sole is Dover Sole, and the name is capitalized by restauranteurs to indicate it is sole de luxe. Other similar, good though not quite so good flat fish go under the names—incorrectly—of Torbay sole and lemon sole. Apart from its flavor, sole keeps as well as any fish will keep away from the sea, which makes it the best British saltwater fish to eat inland. Sole is also, I believe, the only fish that does not smell during cooking. Not only are there numerous ways of cooking sole, but sole has also inspired many sauces. One London restaurant, famous for its seafood, lists on its menu Dover Sole cooked in 54 different ways.

Other flat fish, though eaten commonly enough, fall far below the soles, as their price indicates. Turbot, a larger and rounder fish, heads the rearguard. Halibut, largest of the family, ranks next, though the kindest thing I have heard an Englishman say of it is that it makes a change from cod. Plaice, also larger than the soles, is, as its name might imply, the least interesting of the flats.

On the other hand, all of Britain's shell-fish are hard to surpass. They include, as may be supposed, the lobster and crab, the prawn and shrimp, the oyster and the scallop. And there is the crayfish, a small fresh-water lobster and, confusingly, the crawfish, a rocky or spiny lobster which is caught in abundance along the coasts of Devon and Cornwall. The crawfish is an excellent shell-fish but less popular than it deserves to be. It has no claws—considered the best part of the common lobster—but in compensation the body meat of the crawfish is more tender, and there is more of it.

English oysters, as I've noted, have been appreciated for a long, long time. To understand that well-worn catch-phrase "The Romans ate the natives," you must know that "natives" is the Englishman's popular name for oysters spawned and bred on Kentish or Essex beds. The pick of the lot are Colchester Pyefleets and Royal Whitstables, and of these I say with the Romans that there are no finer oysters anywhere.

Colchester Pyefleets come from the fattest of all oyster fattening grounds, Pyefleet Creek. It lies within the four-and one-half square miles of the great Colne fishery, from where the Romans sent oysters to Rome. It was Richard the Lion-hearted, while king (1189-1199) who, in confirmation of previous rights, gave to the Borough of Colchester, the coastal and capital city of Essex, exclusive rights to the Colne fishery, which was like presenting it with a monopoly in pearls.

The oysters of Whitstable, one of the coastal cities of Kent, are hardly less famous. The Whitstable oyster industry is over two thousand years old. Of recent years, however, some Whitstable oysters have had to be relaid or transplanted from French Brittany, and Whitstable "natives" are now in short supply. They are known as Royal Whitstables, and The Company of Free Fishers and Dredgers of Whitstable alone have the right to call their oysters royal. This company has existed for centuries, membership being an hereditary right enjoyed by the eldest sons of freemen dredgers of Whitstable.

The native English oyster, whether Colchester, Whitstable, or from any other Essex or Kentish bed, should always be eaten uncooked, or as M. Andre L. Simon says, "unspoilt by its beard being removed or palate-paralysing vinegars and sauces added to it. A squeeze of lemon is said to be permissible, but it is the thin end of the wedge of heresy." And the right accompaniment of raw oysters is brown bread with butter, and a glass of Guinness.

It is a common understanding that, above all things, oysters must be very fresh, and with that rigid aim, all oysters sold on the London market must pass stringent tests imposed by the Fishmongers' Company. One cannot help but wonder how the "natives" exported to Rome might have fared had there been a similar company of Roman fishmongers.

The European scallop differs from the American at least in three respects. It is much larger, and contains a "coral," which is absent in the American scallop. The coral is considered the most delicate part, and is the product of the third difference: the European scallop is bi-sexual, or both male and female. At one time the scallop was the centerpiece of many elaborate shell-fish dishes that European chefs loved to dream up for their courts and kings; the kings are no longer so numerous, but scallops continue to play an important part in a fine sea-pie, in company with mussels, prawns, crabs and lobsters. Scallops are also excellent when served alone and in plebian simplicity: poached in their shells, cooked in butter, and sprinkled with chives and chopped parsley.

Because of their size, the shells of European scallops may be used again and again (after a good scrubbing and boiling) as individual dishes. Fireproof as any Pyrex, they offer an attractive touch to made-up or left-over fish dishes. The shells have, in fact, made the scallop the best advertised of all shell-fish. The trademark of the great Shell oil company with its world-wide interests is a scallop shell. As a symbol and decoration in art and architecture, "the pilgrim's shell" has been used from time immemorial.

There are plenty of oddities along the British coastline besides the shell-fish already listed. Among the company that creep and crawl, that open and shut with the turn of the tide, are the whelks and winkles and the pennywinkles; the lamprey, lampern and the limpets; the mussels and the cockles. No wonder that an old fisherman once exclaimed "all that's not cockles nor mussels we call clams," though, in fact, there is no true English clam and American clamming must be foresworn for British cockling.

Of this miscellany, cockles and mussels take precedence, good in place of oysters in fish soup or sauce.

Lastly, your true Englishman since the days of the Druids has relished the little pink bewhiskered shrimp. It is included among the top-prized shell-fish in company with the prawn, the lobster and the crab, for the shrimp has a distinction above all shell-fish. It is the only fish that may be eaten fresh for tea; and in company with anchovy and bloater paste, pounded into its own paste with butter, it also makes a very proper tea-time sandwich or bread-and-butter spread. Shrimp Teas are one of the joys of seaside holidays.

No recipes are given here for fish, since fish is prepared and served more or less in the same way the world over. With these exceptions: the various uses of herring and the dish known as kedegree, are described in Chapter II, under "breakfast" fish; the anchovy and shrimp pastes are described in Chapter XII under savouries.

Hereford cattle

6. Rare, Medium or Well-Done

> Oh! the roast beef of England
> And old England's roast beef.*

HEREFORDSHIRE, WHERE I WAS BORN and spent my braids-and-rib-
bons days, gave mankind its most savored steak. Half of the beef
cattle raised in America are Herefords: their conquest of the
Texas longhorn and lesser bovines is a saga that rivals the vanish-
ing of the plains buffalo herds. And America is but a sector of the

* Henry Fielding, *The Grub Street Opera.*

sprawling domain of these white-faced terra cotta cattle that, wherever I go, remind me of our mutual origin.

Almost wholly rural, fertile and well-fed, Herefordshire is a western Border County; that is, it rubs elbows with Wales. The roast beef of old England is but one prized yield of its rich red soil. Some of England's stoutest oaks tower over its rolling, well-manicured countryside; there too grows wheat that in my father's time fetched the top price on the London market, good quality hops, and orchard after orchard of fine apples.

Ladye Grove, old Aunt Mary's house, looked down from the slopes of Birley Hill on the very heartland of this lush country, or so it will always seem to me. From there I could see Birley, my father's old home, and the family farming acres: the country around my mother's home The Hyde, and the watermill where the wheat was ground for bread; and the neighboring hamlets of Canon and King's Pyon where Benjamin Tomkins, originator of the Hereford cattle, started breeding for beef with his two cows, Pigeon and Mottle, in 1742. I saw it as a panorama of grass orchards and hopyards, thick pastures and strong-colored arable land, little wooded hills, and beyond, the distant heather-covered ridge of Radnor Forest.

In my grandfather's day the red and white Hereford "pottery cow" was a usual adornment of the cottage mantlepiece; the ox, roasted whole in the market square, was the accepted centerpiece at feasts and festivals and public celebrations of great events. Herefordshire men were almost all country men, for the most part yeomen—yeomen farmers.

The English yeoman is, in fact, the common ancestor of nearly every Englishman, though modern life has become congested in towns. Until the beginning of the Industrial Revolution, the yeoman was a freeman of the rustic world who earned his living, in one way or another, from the soil. Above all he was independent, and the backbone of old England's prosperity in peace and strength in war. He followed the flag to wherever and whatever it led.

He was always a serving man, but voluntarily so—had he not been a freeman since the beginning of Elizabeth I's long reign, or earlier! He was the master of the long-bow, the weapon before which the proudest knights of France had bowed in defeat at the Battle of Crecy in 1346. He was the man to whom Shakespeare's Henry V appealed at Agincourt, when he wanted to muster the full valor of his fighting men:

> *you good yeomen*
> *Whose limbs were made in England show us here*
> *The mettle of your pasture.*

It is still a commonplace wherever English is spoken to say of some favorite tool, or well-worn jacket, or faithful old car: "It did me yeoman's service." That expression means in our Atomic Age precisely what it did when Benjamin Tomkins, with the help of Pigeon and Mottle, was starting mankind on its way toward the best of all steaks and roast beef.

Good beef was an alloy of the "mettle" of a yeoman's pasture. No less than a Grand Duke of Tuscany so noted in 1669 when, after inspecting the yeomen of The King's Body Guard, he described those husky fellows as "great eaters of beef, of which a very large ration is given them daily at the court, and they might be called beef-eaters."

Now, the pottery cow is a collector's item; the feasts over the whole ox-roast in the square are no more. Mainly in memory and tale survive such one-time pillars of London life as the Beefsteak Clubs: one of 1735 vintage bore the imposing name of The Sublime Society of Steaks, and its members were The Steaks. The Beef-Eaters of the Guard have become a recruitment of old soldiers who serve as Yeomen Warders under the Constable of the Tower of London, and it has been a long time, verily a long time, since any Englishman received "a very large ration" of beef daily.

But Britain is still the home and the stronghold of prime quality beef, while the Hereford white-faced steers, and in lesser numbers, the Short-Horn and the Aberdeen Angus, all British beef-breeds, dot the earth's pasturelands—call these beeves, though you smile, the new flags of empire.

It is now the Dominions of the British Commonwealth, and well-fed Americans, who out-eat all others, even Englishmen, when beef is the *pièce de resistance* at dinner. In the United States, for instance, your Western ranch-owner quite casually, as a routine duty on behalf of his ever-filled larder, butchers a whole beef for storage in his "deep freeze"; in him the yeoman of yore has found a worthy successor. The popular out-door barbecue was once the ritual of the feudal castle's courtyard, then of the Great Plains where cow-country men roasted their beef in an earthy pit. The ancient Saxons, however, preceded them all as the original chefs of the live coal fire and grate under the stars.

The British, you see, have had centuries on end in which to make up their minds and palates on just how to cook their meats, on what are the best cuts and the best ways to prepare and garnish them. Their eleventh-century Norman conquerors not only added beauty to the countryside by their abbeys and monasteries, but they introduced a civility to Saxon England, a refinement to Saxon food.

The Norman lords brought along their own Norman French cooks, who promptly recruited Saxons to serve as underlings and become cooks for the cooks as well as scullions. So the Saxon helpers learned new flavorings, new dishes, new ways of making their own plain fare more relishable, and in turn added refinements of their own as the old chore became an art. This Norman French influence blended with the Saxon down-to-earthness provides the motif to the whole of English cookery, which is simplicity plus taste.

It also explains an oddity in the language of English food: the use of the French word for the meat, and retention of the Saxon word for the animal—beef, from the French *boeuf* for the meat of the ox, cow or bull; mutton for the sheep, pork for the pig, veal for the calf. Moreover, though the choice cuts of beef are known by their Norman-French name, sirloin, rib of beef, etc., the less choice tidbits that were left by the Norman lords to their Anglo-Saxon underlings, have kept their original Anglo-Saxon ox prefix—or ox tongue, ox tail, and on down the list.

A baron of beef, the noblest joint, consists of both sirloins cooked and carved, uncut from the backbone. Nowadays only the most expert chef undertakes to roast a baron, usually upon a spit, for great banquets—for many years a baron of beef has been a feature of the banquets served at the Guildhall in the City of London. Even the ten-to-twelve pound sirloin is now, for most families, a thing of the past. Luckily, however, I can savor, in retrospect, our Sunday dinner sirloin, which was almost as much a ritual among us as the Sunday going-to-church. Roasted, entirely, perfectly and simply, and as simply served, invariably tidbits accompanied it. Not what the old Anglo-Saxon thought of as tidbits, but the extras and garnishings without which roast beef was unthinkable. They included greens, which is the general word for such members of the cabbage tribe as brussels sprouts, kale and sprouting broccoli; roast potatoes, clear sizzling hot gravy, horse-radish, and for the tidbit climax, Yorkshire pudding.

This famous pudding, a combination of flour and eggs, has long been the established English accompaniment to roast beef— only in Yorkshire the beef is regarded as the accompaniment to the pudding. Though Yorkshire pudding is good with any meat, the purists say that it should rightly be served only with ribs or rounds of beef, and they but grudgingly concede it to be served with sirloin.

The horse-radish at our Sunday dinner was not served in the form of sauce, but shredded, fresh and white as driven snow, and as hot as the hottest mustard to the taste.

Beef dripping was another tidbit—the word "dripping" dates from the days when the old spit-roast was used, and the fat dripping from a joint before the fire fell into a waiting basin. Bread and dripping, sprinkled with salt, was an "elevenses" or mid-morning snack that we relished as children; dripping toast, again with salt, was a nursery tea-time treat.

Veal, however, was something the Saxons never appreciated like the Normans. The frugal Saxon thought it wasteful to kill a calf, and resented the demanding Normans despoiling the herds of Saxon cattle; they saw nothing appetizing either in the brutish Norman method of slaughtering the calves. Thus, over the centuries since, veal has never been what can be called a typical English meat, though in our family, leaning somewhat to the Normans, a roasted round of stuffed veal, and accompanying forcemeat balls and thick gravy, was a regular Whitsunday dish. The most popular use in England for veal is in a veal-and-ham pie which ranks in favor second only to the hard-crust glazed pork pie.

But enough of beef! Second to it, and not always second either, every true son or daughter of Britain relishes the meat of the sheep, and has since Britain was young. Not long ago I read in an American newspaper a headline that smacked of the incredulous: *"An Englishman Insists Mutton Can Be Good."* I stand with the roving epicure who inspired the headline, and valiantly stood his ground. Mutton is good; indeed, well-cooked it is delicious. In testimony to that solid fact a surprising number of England's literary great have been eloquent in praise both of mutton and lamb. Sam Weller of Dicken's *Pickwick Papers,* for one, enjoyed nothing better than his boiled leg of mutton with caper sauce.

It is quite easy to understand why English cooks prepare mutton so well, and why English trenchermen are so partial to the good fare offered by the sheep, if you venture into the history of the wool trade in Britain, and such famed by-products of it as Irish Stew, Lancashire Hot Pot, and Shepherd's Pie.

Wool was "the flower and strength and revenue and blood of England" * until the development of the cotton trade, towards the end of the eighteenth century. Wool was the first source of

* *Encyclopaedia Britannica,* 1911.

England's prosperity and the foundation of her commercial strength. The great Cistercian abbeys of Herefordshire and Gloucestershire and the north of England bear witness to the men who first grew the wool, pasturing their sheep upon the hillsides of the Severn and Wye Valleys and on the Yorkshire dales. The splendid churches of the Cotswolds and East Anglia are equally elegant reminders of the profits of the early days of wool manufacturing. Visit Parliament, Britain's political holy of holies. The Woolsack—a large square cushion of wool, covered with red cloth—is still the seat of the Lord Chancellor in the House of Lords, set there by Edward III (1327-37) to remind his peers of the importance of the wool trade to the realm.

There was a time when sheep-stealing was rife in England on a scale far more general than cattle-rustling ever attained in the United States. And in those days a sheep-stealer, if caught, had to forfeit his life for a sheep. As late as my grandfather's day, our Birley Hill was a haunt of sheep-stealers. I recall grim tales, told on winter nights, which sent me fearful to bed, of sheep-stealers shooting game-keepers who tried to stop them. In the wood above Ladye Grove was a leafy path that led to a ruined sheep-stealer's cottage, and about that ruin we children felt a silent, foreboding air, as though violence had been done there on many a wild, dark night. In the center of the stone-flagged floor of the cottage was a small iron ring. When the sun was bright enough to fortify our backbones, we crept inside, tugged at the ring and lifted up the square of flagstone; in the opening below we could see the stone steps that led into the roomy cellar where, it was said, the stolen sheep had been hidden.

> *"O the mountain is the sweeter,*
> *But the valley is the fatter;*
> *And so we deem it meeter*
> *To carry off the latter."*

So went an old border-country raiding song. The sheep that had been hidden in that tallow-candlelit cellar to the words of the old song were, no doubt, the Ryeland sheep, small and horn-less with white faces and legs, a Herefordshire breed far older than the Hereford cattle. The Ryeland wool was prized above that of other breeds. It was once the gold mine, the "Lemster Ore," of my home town; the "golden fleece fair Hereford" * that the Earl of Hereford wore at the Battle of Agincourt.

Sheep-stealers, however, didn't risk their lives for a fleece of wool. "Their love o' mutton beat their love o' sheep." ** Wild game abounded and was far easier to hunt down and hide, yet mutton was their choice above most other meats. The Ryelands sheep were nice and plump, well worth raiding from the lush valley pastures for the thieves' cook-pot, though it might cost a man his life.

At The Hyde, a lamb was always killed for Easter. For the annual Hop-picking Supper, when the hops had all been stripped from the binds, some sheep were killed and cooked in the big brick bread-oven. The roasts were then portioned out according to the number in each hop-picker's family, so that some had a big leg and others a small shoulder. In like fashion Christmas pud-dings, big or little, were handed out to top the feast.

In my home, lamb or mutton was served quite as often as beef; perhaps on balance we ate more mutton. For beast by beast, sheep offer far more diversity in food than beef cattle. A roast saddle or shoulder of either lamb or mutton is an epicurean de-light: roast leg of lamb, and roast or boiled leg of mutton, are close runners-up. Mutton chops, and lamb cutlets; mutton kidneys as entrees, and as *the* kidneys for the popular breakfast dish of kidneys and bacon; old-time mutton pies, these all testify to the diversity of mutton. Moreover, almost all the good traditional "made-up" country meat dishes, such as Lancashire Hot-Pot, Irish Stew, Shepherd's or Cottage Pie, call for mutton in prefer-ence to any other meat. As for economical diversity, nothing equals the weekly joint of mutton, as "Vicarage Mutton" details:

* Michael Drayton, *The Battle of Agincourt*.
** James Russell Lowell, *The Courtin'*.

Hot on Sunday
Cold on Monday,
Hashed on Tuesday
Minced on Wednesday,
Curried Thursday,
Broth on Friday,
Cottage pie Saturday

The old-day Englishman's liking for mutton went hand in hand with his meaty "know-how." He understood the three factors which determine the quality of home-raised lamb and mutton: breed, age, and feeding. Blindfolded he could tell the difference between Mountain and Down sheep, as the sheep-stealers' song notes that difference; and any competent housewife knew that she could not treat all types of mutton alike. Accordingly, the Victorian butcher, to please customers and thus maintain his trade, prided himself above all on the conditioning of mutton, for his customers knew when mutton was prime mutton and not dressed as lamb. Prime mutton was from a sheep four years old, lean and well-flavored by proper feeding; and lamb ceased to be lamb when it was one year old. Nowadays, with much of England's meat imported, more people eat "caponed" lamb, which is in reality a two-year old mutton, than may be guessed.

The reliable modern butcher knows his mutton, if most of the public do not, and he will serve you better if you ask specifically for Southdown lamb or Southdown mutton. The Southdowns are raised on the aromatic grass of the chalk downs of southern England, and today are the top sheep for meat. Insist on Southdown and you will have as good a feast as a sheep-stealer once thought was worth his life.

I bow to the Southdown, but my own preference is for the small Welsh sheep that graze the wild thyme and short grass of the hillsides of Wales. Delicate, sweet, not so fat and well-hung, a saddle of mutton from the Welsh hills is worth going far to find. I agree with George Borrow that "the leg of mutton of Wales beats the leg of mutton of any other country," and like him "I shall never forget the first Welsh leg of mutton which I tasted, rich but delicate, replete with juices derived from the aromatic herbs . . . cooked to a turn, and weighing just four pounds." *

Just as beef in its various cooked forms has its traditional asides, so do mutton and lamb. The "musts" for roast lamb are green peas, new potatoes sprinkled with fine-chopped parsley and anointed with melted butter, and of course mint sauce. A roast leg of mutton is certainly much less than it deserves to be if it lacks onion sauce and red currant jelly. Boiled mutton demands caper sauce.

Beef, lamb or mutton, if properly roasted in the first place, can be almost as good when served cold as hot, in which case good pickles and fresh salad are traditional companions. At home we always had four pickle jars on the go, glass-stoppered, with their long-handled pickle-forks beside them. There was red cabbage pickle; pickled onions, and mustard pickles, generally known as Piccalilli. Mustard pickles, varying in minor ingredients, consist in the main of cucumbers, onions, and small, broken pieces of cauliflower blended with mustard and tumeric and are probably one of the oldest condiments of English country housewives. The great Qualiotti who was Napoleon Bonaparte's personal Chef before he came to England, originated mustard pickles' commercial counterpart for the House of Crosse & Blackwell, naming it Piccalilla. Other pickles, beside this standby four, were reserved as exclusive additions to the accompaniments of cold mutton—small white pickled onions, pickled mushrooms and pickled damsons—since the pickles for mutton should rightly contain a green or a fruit element. Colman's "English" mustard is permanently allied with prime beef, just as mint sauce is with lamb, either hot or cold. Although mint jelly is preferred in Canada and the United States, mint sauce is the Englishman's choice; in fact it is an English culinary monopoly. The recipes for the sauces and the condiments to accompany these meats are described in a later chapter.

* George Borrow, *Wild Wales*.

As for the "made-up" meat dishes that I have mentioned in passing, a few deserve more attention. The best-known among them favors beef; the remainder, mutton.

Beefsteak and kidney pudding may be found on the menu of most inns and restaurants that feature native British cooking. The *Cheshire Cheese* in Wine Office Court, a small alley-way off London's Fleet Street, famous for its association with Dr. Johnson two hundred years ago, is almost as famous today for its steak-kidney-and-mushroom pudding. This is served at lunch time through the cold days of autumn and winter, and is carved in the dining room by the head waiter.

Lancashire Hot Pot, especially liked in the north of England, is another traditional winter dish, often taking the place of Irish stew, which it much resembles. The hot pot is best described as a stew baked in the oven, and for both hot pot and Irish stew, mutton is the meat preferred as the main ingredient. Apart from chicken or prawn and other such curries, where butcher's meat is used, it should be mutton.

A "mince" may be as insipid as the word, but minced mutton, well seasoned, and made up into Shepherd's Pie can be very tasty indeed. And so are rissoles, a dish more than three hundred years old; it is a dish of minced mutton or beef made up into little savory balls that are fried to a crisp, golden brown.

Mixed Grill is properly not a made-up dish at all, but an assortment of several meats and condiments; it is a testing dish for the cook because of the need to allow the correct frying time to each of its meats. The English Mixed Grill consists usually of a grilled lamb cutlet, a sausage, and kidney and tomato; it is served plain but accompanied by a choice of bottled sauces. But if you make such additions as curls of bacon and mushrooms, the grill becomes one of the best of dishes.

Cornish pasty deserves special mention. It looks like an apple turnover but holds beefsteak. Years without number it has been a country supper standby of Cornwall, and makes an ideal complete-course picnic meal, since the correct way to eat Cornish pasty is to hold it in your hand. It is commonly served in Cornish inns, and has found its way to the United States by way of the Cornish miners who once thronged to the copper mines about Lake Superior. Roadside stands thereabouts today peddle Cornish pasties instead of Hot Dogs.

Beef, mutton, the pig! These three are the traditional meats of England. Great is beef, greater is mutton, but greatest is the pig, as next we shall see.

Sam Weller

Beefsteak and Kidney Pudding

For a medium-sized pudding, use a basin that holds approximately 1½ pints of water.

Make a pastry of:

1 lb. of flour
6 oz. of butter, or beef suet finely minced.
½ pint of water
½ teaspoonful salt

(This pastry should be on the moist side).

Filling:

1 lb. of beefsteak, cut into convenient pieces
2-4 sheep's kidneys, skinned.

These should be sprinkled and shaken in a dusting of flour, pepper and salt.

Grease the basin, and line it with the pastry, leaving a piece for the lid.

Put the meat in the pudding, and pour in ¼ pint of water, or enough to fill the basin almost to the top.

Place the pastry lid on top. Firm the edges of the lining and the lid carefully together, to prevent steam escaping.

Tie the pudding basin in a floured cloth (a sheet of wax-paper securely tied will answer as a makeshift).

Simmer in a saucepan for 3-4 hours.

The pudding is served in the basin, with a napkin tied round it when ready for the table.

Mushrooms and oysters are excellent additions to this recipe, which is for a plain beefsteak and kidney pudding.

Rissoles

"Risshe shewes," as they were called in the fifteenth century, are savory meat balls, of cold meat cut up finely or put through a mincer.

Season the cut-up or minced meat rather highly with fresh

green herbs, such as parsley and chives. Shape into small
balls, binding them with a beaten egg. Roll into breadcrumbs and egg, and fry briskly.

Cold potatoes, mashed and seasoned and made into balls,
are good accompaniments, and the whole should be served
with a well-flavored gravy.

Lancashire Hot Pot

Hot Pot is a stew cooked in the oven. Popular in the north of
England, it often takes the place of—and resembles—Irish Stew.
A deep fireproof oven dish with a lid is used, and sold in England
as a Hot Pot; by preference a brown earthenware dish should
be used.

Any kind of meat can be used to make this dish, but mutton
is far the best. By tradition, hot pots should contain kidneys and
oysters and mushrooms, and be accompanied by red cabbage
pickle. A plain hot pot contains only meat and vegetables arranged in layers.

2 lbs. best end of neck of mutton

2 sheep's kidneys

1 oz. dripping

1 onion

1 oz. flour

¾ pint hot stock

4 or 5 mushrooms

1 doz. oysters

2 lbs. of potatoes

Cut the meat into neat cutlets, trimming off nearly all the fat.

In a separate pan, heat the dripping and brown the meat, and
then put this into the Hot Pot.

Brown the onion in the pan. Add the flour, and cook until
brown.

Add the hot stock, stir into the flour, as in making gravy.
Season with salt and pepper and a light sprinkling of sugar.

Slice the kidney thickly over the cutlets.

Add the mushrooms, and then the oysters, so as to form
separate layers.

Cut the peeled potatoes in thick slices so as to make a potato
roof like over-lapping tiles.

Pour in the stock until almost level with the potatoes.

Bake with the lid on in a good moderate oven for 2 hours.

Take the lid off during the last 20 minutes baking, so that
the top layered potato slices may be crisp and brown.

Irish Stew

1 lb. mutton (neck of mutton)
2 lbs. potatoes
½ lb. onion
¼ pint of water

Cut meat off the large bones in small, neat, thick slices, leaving the cutlet and similar bones with the meat on them.

Peel and slice potatoes thickly, and cut each slice in halves.

Put a layer of meat at the bottom of the saucepan. Sprinkle
over a layer of onions, then a thick layer of potato. Season
all with pepper and salt. Pour the water over all and put
on the lid. Bring gently to simmering point, and cook for
2½ hours or longer—the longer the better.

Stir frequently to prevent burning on to the saucepan.

The secret of making Irish Stew is to add as little water as
possible, just enough to give the meat and vegetables a start.
Cooking in their own juices, the meat is embedded in a thick
gravy, with all liquid absorbed.

Cornish Pasty

½ lb. flour
3 oz. lard or dripping
a pinch of salt
water to make a fine dough—about ¼ pint.

Filling:

½ *lb. uncooked beef steak*   1 *medium turnip*
¼ *lb. uncooked calf's liver*   2 *small carrots*
2 *uncooked potatoes*   *pepper and salt*
1 *large onion*

Roll out the dough fairly thin, and cut into squares.

Chop steak and liver finely. Mix together, and season.

Peel, scrape and slice the potato, onion and turnip and carrot. Mix and season.

Put a layer of vegetables on half of each square of pastry, with some of the chopped meat on top.

Brush edges of pastry with white of egg.

Fold the plain half of pastry over the meat, and pinch the edges well together.

Bake 1 hour, at first in good oven to raise the pastry, and then in a very moderate oven to cook the meat and vegetables.

It is important to close the edges neatly and closely, so that no steam escapes, and to use uncooked meat and vegetables.

This recipe makes 2 large or 3 medium-sized pasties.*

Cottage Pie or Shepherd's Pie

Take mutton from a cold joint, and put it through a mincer.

Season well with herbs, onions, salt and pepper, and a few drops of Worcestershire sauce.

Mix in a little good jellied stock—sufficient to moisten the meat throughout.

Top with mashed potatoes beaten up with a very little hot milk, butter, pepper and salt.

Spread the potato crust evenly, and score into dice.

Bake in a hot oven until the surface is nicely browned, and serve with stewed tomatoes.

* Florence White, *Good Things in England*, 1932.

Every cottager kept a pig

7. The Gentleman Who Pays the Rent

> "Look at Pork. There's a subject!
> If you want a subject, look at Pork!"

SO ENTHUSED CHARLES DICKENS IN *Great Expectations*. Charles Lamb foreran him with his noble essay, *A Dissertation Upon Roast Pig*. As a plodder in their footsteps, I rise to the challenge by according The Pig a chapter to himself.

John Bull's praise of England's roast beef has been deep, loud and fervent, and sheep-stealing, as we've seen, carried the penalty of death, yet throve. However, if the men of old had been as statistically prone as we are, I've little doubt that the columns of figures would own to the truth that Englishmen once ate more pig—or hog, if you will—than any other meat. And it is my guess that truth still holds.

Time Magazine recently calculated that Britons daily eat enough "bangers," the affectionate term for pork sausages, to stretch end on end from Lands End to the tip of Scotland, and still have enough bangers left over to give one apiece to every human residing in the American state of Delaware. *Time* did not venture to estimate the immense quantities of bacon and ham that are consumed by Englishmen for breakfast alone, and the items so far mentioned barely introduce the resources of the hog when tapped to the last squeal.

No less than the Herefords and other of Britain's famous breeds of beeves and sheep, the English breeds of pigs now root and forage their way in boundless pens and pastures abroad. Their lineage is as ancient, or more so, as that of the proudest duke-doms, and their very names ring to magic notes: the Large White Yorkshire, the little Welsh pig, the sandy Tamworth, the showy Gloucester Old Spots. And by no means least, the Berkshire, descendant of a mediaeval rooter, whose warm brown hue blends with the colors of the beech woods where he loves most to fatten himself; the hardy black and white Essex, scion of the half-wild swine that roamed the deep forests and marshes of Essex before the days of gunpowder.

British "home-cured" ham and bacon are now, alas, in the same rare category as home-made bread and farmhouse butter. But at least until the first World War, life for a countryman—a squire, a farmer, or a cottager—was almost unthinkable in England without the home-grown pig. For the country housewife the killing of the pig was the great event in the domestic year.

Before a law was passed that forbids the keeping of pigs near a dwelling, every cottager kept a pig hard by under his own eye. The pig was the corner-stone of his economy, to be watched, favored, guarded; it ruled his diet the year through, supplied him with lard for the winter puddings and pies, brawns and sausages, as well as his ham and bacon, roast pork, chops, and what-not. The pig, to the countryman, was the gentleman who paid the rent.

> "To have a sty in the garden, or, as often, abutting on the cottage, was held to be as essential to the happiness of a newly married couple as a living room or a bedroom. So much was the pig a part of domestic life that no vision was satisfactory that did not include the flitch of bacon on the wall of the living room, and hams and gammons hanging from the ceiling." *

* Walter Rose, *Good Neighbours*, 1942.

The good old Saxon word "larder" reflects the ancient importance of the pig. Your English larder of yore was, until the refrigerator ousted it, the essential cold store-room for food of every house, built facing north, the floor stone-flagged, the walls fitted with lead slabs and wooden shelves, and adjacent to the kitchen. But before the larder attained so stalwart a character it was nothing but a tub of lard, a bowl perhaps, set in the kitchen cupboard. As times improved, the cupboard became a room, and the room kept the lard tub's name. It became the larder.

Except in short-lived periods of extreme heat—rare in England —when it is difficult to keep milk and butter over-long, the larder is more serviceable in the insular climate than is the best refrigerator. The larder may not keep things fresh quite as long, but it keeps them better; it never commits the sacrilege of ruining good pastry, never robs any food of its flavor. Faithfully it protects and also preserves what is the best in bread, butter, milk; what makes for taste in the cold meats and the pies and puddings and tarts. And this King's Guard over stored foods' excellence all began with a tub of lard, that all-important by-product of the source of England's most cherished meat, The Pig.

A story was told during World War II to dramatize the almost holy regard that is held by your English countryman for bacon. Rationing after the war was a dreary ordeal in prospect, and a Herefordshire farmer, so the story went, decided to forestall any such tragedy for himself, his wife, and small son.

The farmer owned a pig. Under his care, which was as that of a doting parent, the pig grew to 100 pounds, when it became what is known as a "pork pig." At 220 pounds, it became a "bacon pig," yet the farmer withheld the knife; he continued to stuff the animal with the best meal the miller would allow him.

The pig's weight went to 300 pounds, to 400 pounds, then to 500 pounds, when it became a "ham pig." By all the rules of good husbandry, no pig could attain a higher ranking than ham pig, but still the farmer plied it with meal and patient care.

At last the miller stopped by. There wasn't enough meal at his mill, he told the farmer, to satisfy a man who did not know when a pig had had enough. By then the pig tipped the scales at over a quarter of a ton.

"It's a worse war than the other," said the farmer.

"It is," the miller granted, "but what has stuffing a pig beyond all sound sense to do with the war?"

"Bacon rationing," said the farmer. "I reckon that we're in for a good fifteen years of it. On rations of four ounces of bacon per head per week, the pig is now only big enough to keep me, the wife and son in bacon for twelve years and three months. He's got to grow big enough to supply two years and nine months more."

The miller, too, was a lover of good Herefordshire home-grown bacon, and soon was fattening up a post-war ration pig of his own, just to be on the safe side at breakfast.

In the good old days, all pigs were usually larger and fatter, big enough to insure an ample supply well ahead. Methods of curing and salting down the meat varied from one locality to another. This, with the diversity in the breeds of pigs, produced a toothsome diversity of "home" hams and bacons. Wiltshire, Devon and Somerset, Norfolk, Lancashire and Durham bacons, each had its special points of favor; the York ham and the Suffolk flitch were distinctively different local prides. Today's mass-curing by the big bacon packers has rubbed out many such fine distinctions, at the big packers' cost; they must now compete on their own home ground with Danish bacon, and to a lesser extent with Polish, Dutch, Hungarian and Irish bacon.

At home we relied for our home-cured hams and bacon on one of the Birley farms, the Lower Hill. I remember its dwelling as the quintessence of the old farmhouse: a centuries-old black and white farmhouse with stone-flagged steps and floors, and the door lintel so low that the men stooped to enter it. It was surrounded by an orchard of a few damson but mostly apple trees. The farmer's wife, Mrs. Millichip, presided over the low-raftered kitchen with its bright red geraniums on the window-sills, hams and bacon hanging from the rafters, and there was always something cooking on the old-style wood range. Mrs. Millichip was kitchen-wise, her recipes stored in her memory; she was wise, too, in her "knowing" use of herbs and spices, and she knew every in-and-out date of the farming and hunting year. All the pig meat, and we had it in great variety, went through Mrs. Millichip's careful scrutiny, though the pies and brawn were made, and the hams and bacon cured and stored, under our own roof.

Bacon formerly meant pork: today it means only the back and sides of a pig after the slabs have been cured and smoked. Bacon alone, or bacon and eggs, as I've shown, comprise the great British breakfast dish, with liver or kidneys, tomatoes or mushrooms and potatoes often the accompaniments of the breakfast bacon. But there are other times to eat bacon too. For picnics on the heather-covered Radnorshire hills we used to peel the long slender hazel sticks, point one end, and use them as toasting forks to frizzle rashers of bacon over the open wood-fire. We let hot bacon drippings enriched by the double wood-smoke curing, soak into our bread. Hot boiled bacon was served with boiled fowl; cold boiled bacon, plus a little mustard, scullions and whole crisp lettuce leaves, provided an ever popular luncheon dish.

English hams, despite the big packers or because of their care, have retained much of the individuality that bacon has lost. York Ham is universally popular today; tender, mild, attractively pink, the original Yorkshire ham was smoked with oak sawdust from York Cathedral. Suffolk Ham is sweet-cured. The labels "Wiltshire" and "Bradenham" need explaining. A Wiltshire ham is not necessarily Wiltshire born: technically, it is the leg of the pig cured on the side; while Bradenham ham is not produced, as I used to think, at Bradenham, Buckinghamshire, but is the registered name of the finest of Wiltshire hams. Marketed by the Bradenham Ham Company in Wiltshire, these hams are cured sweet and with milk according to a recipe of 1781, and are then hung up for many months to mature. They are easily recognized by their coal black outside.

The Bath Chap, a cold-meat favorite, is a ham variant which was a specialty of nineteenth-century Bath. It is the lower half of a small pig's head divided and cured with sugar and spices, and dried or smoked like a ham. Exactly as in cooking the home-cured hams, the Bath Chap is soaked first in cold water and then simmered slowly. When well done, the skin is removed, and while still hot is coated with grated breadcrumbs or raspings, then left to cool.

Sausage covers innumerable "tasty little 'bags of mystery'" * mostly of finely chopped and highly seasoned meat bound by such starchy mixers as breadcrumbs. There is no such easy way to recognize the content of the pork sausage as there is with the Bradenham ham. Anyone who thinks that the British are disinterested in food should know something of the controversy that has raged in recent years around the postwar English "banger." As one Minister of Agriculture admitted in Parliament: "I find the sausage to be a much more complex entity than I had ever imagined," adding ruefully, "very deep passions are aroused by this subject."

During the lean years, true English pork sausage was sadly debased, its meat content so lowered that a music-hall comic cried: "What should I put on this, marmalade or mustard?" Though familiarity breeds acceptance, and though no one in England under thirty years old can remember what the pre-war "banger" was like, there lately have been continual mutterings and protests for a better and a meatier sausage. Even London's staid *Times* has drooled in pre-war memory as it speculated on what the return of the old-style sausage might be like.

> "Shall we still like it best when its skin has taken on a beautiful blackness, with a little pink bud peeping through the crack? Will it taste most distinctively divine at a long, lazy Sunday breakfast, or at luncheon while reposing on its cushion of mashed potatoes?"

* Andre L. Simon, *Guide to Good Food and Wines,* 1956.

The smouldering mutterings blazed into vociferous controversy in 1957, at the Brussels Fair, when the Belgians denied the caterers of the "typical English pub" in the British pavilion the right to serve British sausages on the ground that they were not, by Belgian standards, classed as meat. The pride of Britain was stung. Though the Government still refused, in the face of such an international scandal, to set a definite standard for pork sausage, the snub at least led to a belated spirit of reform among sausage makers. One company promptly produced an old-style pork sausage as "a luxury sausage"; of prime leg of pork with egg only used for binding, and flavored with a secret flavoring described as "superb and nostalgic." The price of this luxury of gone days is high, but a surprising number of the British people are willing to pay the difference to get back to the ordinary fare of their grandparents.

The truth about the sausage is summed up by one of Mrs. Millichip's sage sayings: "It ain't what you do, it's the way how you do it. That's what gets results." Her secret for flavoring sausage was time-proved salt and pepper, mace and sage, and maybe "just a touch" of ginger.

The big sausage makers—one of them uses 10,000 pigs a week for a country-wide market—now can prove to you that nutritionally their post-war product is superior to the venerated pre-war product. But in trying to please everyone, they have succeeded in pleasing few with their flavorless compromises. Sausages are properly a meat, not a vegetarian dish, but high meat content alone does not produce a savory sausage—not as I recall Mrs. Millichip's masterpiece. The judicious use of fresh, finely grated breadcrumbs is perfectly permissible, by some preferred, and taste should vie with nutriment. In pre-war days, sausages differed district by district according to the locally preferred herb flavorings, much as hams and bacon differed according to their curing. The South, for instance, preferred a spicy, peppery sausage; the North, a softer, sage flavor. There is no such thing as a sausage that will suit everybody's palate.

Mrs. Millichip was the source of quite another tasty little bag of mystery, an oatmeal sausage which we called groats. It was peculiar, I think, to the Welsh Borderland, though oddly I never heard of it outside our family, and have found only one reference to it in books. We loved groats so well that the dish proved for one of my brothers, long abroad, to be among the best-remembered items of the "food back home." When he returned from years spent in India, his first request dish was groats.

Made of coarse oatmeal, or groats, of lard, chopped onions or leeks, this specialty was flavored with thyme and marjoram, or organy, as Mrs. Millichip called it, and put into sausage skins. Mrs. Millichip regarded organy as *the* essential flavoring, and I've little doubt that it gave her groats such high rating with us. Her organy, I suspect, was the wild, native marjoram gathered in our fields, for the wild variety differs slightly in flavor from the cultivated.

There are all sorts of sausage variations, but it is time to strike out for the Midlands and Melton Mowbray Pie, the Pie of Pork Pies. That favorite hunting country with its great grass fields and blackthorn and quickset hedges has also given the world Stilton cheese; if its Pie has not traveled so widely it is only because pork pie is not a good keeper: it must be fresh to be at its best, and that best is the Midlands' traditional fare.

Every English farmhouse and inn once had its own recipe for pork pie, but generations of keen-palated travelers by stagecoach could not abstain from an undisputed truth. Local pride aside, Melton Mowbray Pie towered above the ablest competition, which was saying much in a land of first-rate pork pies.

Many cooks have sought to ferret out the secret of the Midlands' triumphant pie. Its supremacy is probably in part due to the dash of anchovy essence that is added to the flavoring ingredients; that extra touch also makes the inside of the pie a pinkish color instead of the usual brown. One dessertspoonful of the essence will do the trick for nine pounds of pork. And if you wish a real Melton Mowbray Pie, you will see to it that one-third of your pork's weight is fat. Nine pounds of pork will make six goodly pies.

Like sausages, pork pies are now big business. The leading pork-pie specialist on grand scale is Saxby Brothers Limited, of the Midlands shire of Northampton. The five Saxbys who direct this family enterprise celebrated their first fifty years as meat-pie bakers in 1956, so there can be no question about their memory of real pre-war pork pie. They turn out Melton Mowbray pork pies, and veal-and-ham pies as well, in sizes ranging from five-to-six ounces up to seven pounds—108,000 pies per week, which means over 70,000 pounds of pies by weight. Their Melton Mowbray pie is of glazed brown pastry shaped round and deep, whereas its running mate, the veal-and-ham pie, is either square or oblong. Friday is Pie Delivery Day. In the wee hours of Friday mornings, like a ritual, a fleet of vans rumble from the Saxby kitchens, the first van departing at the stroke of midnight. The vans deliver the pies to Saxby distributing centers near and far so that the housewife may have her choice of them without fail for the weekend.

In panorama, the pig is at once astounding and ludicrous. The remaining dishes that it so generously provides range from the sublime to the ridiculous, with some humdrum in between. According to Charles Lamb, roast pork—English-style, of course—belongs to the sublime. Contrary to the accepted practice of the rest of Europe, the English cook leaves the outer skin on the pork for "crackling." The skin is cut into thin strips as deep as the first layer of fat, and the joint is thrust into a hot oven to sizzle before the heat is reduced. Served with apple sauce and roast potatoes, the rich reddish crackling adds zest to the finished roast, which is excellent when eaten either hot or cold.

Roast suckling pig and boar's head might be placed in the category of ridiculous dishes, and though they once graced the festive boards of kings are almost as rare today as a baron of beef. I once feasted on roast suckling pig at an Essex farm in wartime, when a sow and her breed were counted among the casualties of the nightly bombing raids. The baby pigs were under a month old and thus eligible, whole, for the oven. And since a suckling pig must be roasted the day after it is killed, there was nothing to be done except share the litter with farmer neighbors and reserve one for the home table. Stuffed with sage and onion, the piglet came to table with the traditional small red apple in its mouth, and garnished with sprigs of watercress. Served with sharp apple sauce the meat was rich and meltingly tender and made, especially in wartime, a much enjoyed feast.

As for roast boar's head, I must confess that I have never seen, let alone relished one outside of pictures. Further I must confess that I prefer my pig on the table not to be too suggestive of its departed life. However, long before turkeys were introduced into England, boar's head was the principal offering of the Christmas feast, and that custom is preserved today at The Queen's College, Oxford. There the roasted head is served on a silver platter, decked with rosemary, holly and bays, and with an orange stuck between its formidable front teeth. The only break with tradition is that a domesticated boar, not a wild one, now supplies the head.

The most common use of the boar's head, or of any pig's head, at our old home was as brawn. This is a boned confection of the head meat and other trimmings that is simmered down in herbs, then pressed firmly into a bowl or other mould to cool and set. It was sliced off cold for lunch, and always eaten with mustard and pickles, at times a baked potato.

Galantine is a very similar dish, but with this difference: the meat of brawn is cooked *in* the liquor that forms its jelly, while the meat of galantine is cooked alone and incased or covered with the jelly. In other words, brawn is a blend of meat and jelly, galantine a mixture.

In the sixteenth century, brawn was one of the regular cold plates served to the Lords of the Star Chamber, and before 1200 A.D. "brawne" was a country favorite. The old directions make a point of the need of serving it with mustard—in those days a creamy white sauce made of ground mustard seed, flour, melted lard, and enough good milk to cream the mixture in cooking it. The close American relative to brawn and galantine is the Pennsylvania Dutch creation known as "souse."

Pork and beans go together as naturally as bread and butter, and may fittingly perform our finale for the noble pig. Salt pork cooked with dried beans in winter, and fresh broad beans in spring, have rendered "yeoman service" for Englishmen ever since there has been an England. I've not the slightest doubt that they did their bit for King and Country at Crécy as worthy mates of the long-bow, and so deserve to be named among the founders of democracy.

Groats

1 measure of prepared oatmeal
½ measure of lard
¼ measure of chopped onion, dried herbs—parsley, thyme, sage and marjoram
salt and pepper

Spread the coarse oatmeal on a tray and dry it thoroughly (in the oven or before the fire).

Add the finely chopped lard, onion and herbs. Season with pepper and salt.

Mix all well together, and press into sausage skins, leaving plenty of room for the mixture to swell, as the "stuff" swells considerably in cooking.

Sausages made into a string should be tied with thread, and tied again a half inch from the first knot. This prevents the risk of cutting the sausage skins when the sausages are cut from the string.

Plunge in boiling water and boil 45 minutes. Prick well to avoid bursting. When boiled, hang them up to dry, and they will keep some time after they have dried out.

These sausages are served with bacon in the usual way.

If not intended to keep, the mixture can be fried in pieces, made into little cakes, and not put into sausage skins.

Traditional Sausage Meat

9 lbs. lean pork
3 lbs. firm pork fat
3 lbs. stale bread
Seasonings: 3 oz. salt
*   1 oz. white pepper*
*   ¼ oz. mace*
*   ½ oz. ginger*
*   ¼ oz. ground sage*

One small girl, myself

8. Game and Game Pies

THAT INTERLUDE IN WHICH I grew up between candlelight and electricity, home-cured ham and the packer, was the Indian Summer of the English country gentleman. I speak of him as the symbol of the landed gentry, of the squires who molded four centuries of English history, their heyday being from the reign of William III through that of Queen Victoria.

"First catch your hare before you cook it," was one of the homely maxims of the period; from which it follows that we should get acquainted with the squire and his role before we look into the cook-pot wherein the country housewife prepared so superbly the game that he so jealously guarded on his broad acres to provide the sport and feasts of the hunt.

In most hamlets and villages, the squire was "the lord of the manor." His manor house, which might be elaborate and impressively large, or simple and conveniently modest of size, dominated the landscape as the Normans' abbeys once had done. It was, perhaps, less grand than the seat of a duke, an earl or a baron; the squire may have lacked the glamour of a title; but he was in the greater number, and far more definitely a working, personal force in the community. Liken him to a captain of the line, the titled to the colonels and generals.

In Parliament, the House of Commons was made up almost entirely of country gentlemen, elected by other country gentlemen and their tenants; and it was the House that shaped the course of Britain. On the continent of Europe, the source of governmental power may have been Paris or Berlin or Vienna, the nation's capital; but in the tight little island across the Channel it was the country, not London, that made the laws, whose strong hands held the helm. The hands were the squires'.

Perhaps that is one reason why in Eighteenth Century England the breeding of horses, dogs, cattle, sheep and pigs, largely took the place of war. Breeding fine animals was the over-riding passion of the country gentleman, and it was deep-rooted in his love of country life; in his zest for shooting and hunting, racing and gardening, producing fields of lush farm crops. And since the squires ruled not only their villages but England too, the sittings of Parliament were regulated by the dates of the shooting and hunting seasons. Pursuit of field sports became part of the British way of life, and influenced English social life from top to bottom.

English sporting pictures of the seventeenth and eighteenth centuries—the works of the first truly native school of British painting—give as faithful a picture of that time as do the history books. The library shelves of country houses were loaded with sporting literature, with volumes revolving around the words "fur and feather and fin," rod and gun. Gamekeepers and poachers became national characters; villains or heroes of the piece in turn according to the writer's viewpoint, though public sentiment was always loaded against the harsh, strict, spoil-sport gamekeeper in favor of the cunning, hunt-by-night, law-breaking poacher. Cookery books contained lengthy discourses on the preparation and serving of game—proof that the landed gentry lived off the land. The wild animals and birds that are the object of the chase and whose flesh is used for food provided an epicurean diversity to all English country fare.

To the squires, the pursuit of game was much more than a pastime. It was controlled by strict laws, and probably was the greatest single factor that deepened and lengthened the class-bound society of England. From the reign of Richard II (1377-1389) until 1831, the right of persons other than gamekeepers properly deputed by the lord of a manor to take game was made to depend on the social rank of the person or on the amount of his interest in land. In 1831, the right to kill game was made conditional on the possession of a game certificate, now called a game license.

So powerful was the squires' rule that the enforcement of the Game Laws was left to private enterprise, the arrest of offenders even on the highways being made by the owners or occupiers of the land or their gamekeepers. Not until the Poaching Prevention Act of 1862 were the police given any direct authority over poachers. Poachers were as notorious as highwaymen, and, in districts where private nocturnal war was carried on and owners of sporting rights encountered armed gangs of poachers, there was many a shot in the dark that ended a man's life instead of a rabbit's.

Life for me began at the tail-end of the squires' rule, and life at Birley and Ladye Grove was still lived the squires' way. What Galsworthy wrote of Squire Pendyce and his home of Worsted Skeynes was true of the owners of country houses throughout the land:

> The efforts of social man, directed from immemorial time towards the stability of things, have culminated in Worsted Skeynes. Beyond commercial competition—for the estate no longer paid for living on it—beyond the power of expansion, set with tradition and sentiment, it was an undoubted jewel, past need of warranty. Cradled within it were all those hereditary institutions of which the country was most proud, and Mr. Pendyce sometimes saw before him the time when, for services to his party, he should call himself Lord Worsted, and after his own death continue sitting in the House of Lords in the person of his son. But there was another feeling in the Squire's heart—the air and the woods and the fields had passed into his blood a love for this, his home and the home of his fathers.*

* John Galsworthy, *The Country House*, Putnam, 1907.

Memory of those days, when I went shooting with my father and brothers, of the shooting party days up and over Birley Hill, are now as a series of sporting prints in retrospect. The prints are little different from those that hung in the old-fashioned smoking room at Ladye Grove where the men gathered after a day with guns and dogs and compared notes on the day's sport. Their faces and scenes were my every-day familiars, and through my memory haze of mingling wood-and-tobacco-smoke, I see scores of pictures: my father snipe-shooting, with his unerring aim bringing down a bird as it zigzagged across the frozen tufts of grass that fringed the skating pool; of my eldest brother on the day he shot his first wild duck—a handsome dark-haired lad sitting on the old Windsor kitchen chair, the gun across his knee, the mallard with its iridescent green head dangling down between his legs, and his face flushed with pride and triumph.

There are the still-life pictures: the hares and rabbits; the wood-cock we occasionally shot on Birley Hill, the braces of partridges, and pheasants a limp heap of brown and brilliant metallic feathers, green, blue and yellow, such as Victorian artists liked to portray. There is the large canvas conversation-piece of the annual family shoot on Boxing Day.

Boxing Day is the day after Christmas, a national English holiday and a family day, so called originally after the custom of giving boxes of food and gifts to one's tenants. Nowadays the gifts are given instead to local tradespeople such as the baker and the milkman, the postman and the garbage man.

The family shoot on Boxing Day always started from Ladye Grove. The early morning was all abustle with the crew of beaters gathering, dogs yapping and running round in excited circles, all impatient for the "guns" to move off on the day-long trek across the hill. Behind the scenes, in the kitchen, the big picnic baskets and hampers were filled for the shooters' lunch. And down in the valley the freak white pheasant, whom everyone was ordered never to shoot, moved into the keeper's little garden: a

wise old bird who took his own precaution against any possible
mistaken identity.

All day I stuck to my father's heels as close as any hunting dog,
glad for the way-stops while the beaters did their work. We would
take our stand in the waiting silence, broken at first only by a
rustle in the sodden or frozen undergrowth, and the distant tap-
tap of beaters' sticks against the trees. Then as the beaters worked
nearer, their shouts and tapping grew louder, and all the calm of
the winter morning was shattered by the staccato shot from a gun
as a cock pheasant rose above the spinney, a gleaming brilliance
of whirring wings stopped in mid-flight.

Lunch was invariably eaten under the shelter of an ancient
wide-spreading yew tree atop Birley Hill; a circle of men and
dogs, standing or squatting around the wicker hampers, and one
small girl, myself. From the hampers emerged roast chicken and
ham, a huge sirloin of roast beef, mince pies and cheese together
with butter and loaves of bread. There was a bottle of whisky,
and a quantity of cider that I never got to measure; but all por-
tions in the hampers were more than enough for hungry hunters
and the beaters too.

The daylight would be all but gone by the time we were back
at Ladye Grove. It would be dusk as the day's spoil was distributed from the dog-cart. Under the oil lamps another set of
shooting stories, another set of sporting prints, mingled with the
wood and tobacco smoke of the gun-room. And later in that old
farmhouse we feasted like kings.

Much of the England of my youth was already industrialized,
and only the squires' way of country living could give that ele-
mental unity with the land that we possessed. Of this unity the
game that we hunted and feasted on was a part, as was the display of game hanging in the open-fronted poulterers' shops of
country towns, and even large cities, reflecting the bounty of
England's rural fields and woodlands. The time had then gone
when rooks and four-and-twenty blackbirds were made into a
pie; when larks were roasted on a spit; when flocks of the Great

Bustard [or wild turkey] once rated as the finest English game-bird of all—were a common country sight. But at least we had that Indian Summer, and despite the smoke of factories, some of it is still alive.

Grouse, in Great Britain, means the Red Grouse or Scotch Grouse, which breeds in Scotland and some moorland districts in the north of England, Wales and the West of Ireland. It has a double distinction. Many people regard it, particularly during the two months from mid-August to mid-October of the year when it was fledged, as the king of game. And since all attempts to introduce grouse into other parts of Europe have failed, there is no name for this bird in any other language. Grouse eats as well cold as hot, some think even better, and has a deeper and more individual flavor than any other game bird. For this reason grouse holds the same place among game meats as Stilton cheese holds among cheeses. For the fullest enjoyment of either it should be served for really special occasions, like a rare vintage wine.

The Grey or Common English partridge might be called the favorite game bird of Britain as it is more widely distributed and abundant than either grouse or pheasant. The gourmet ranks the partridge close to grouse, and some even give it precedence over any other English game bird. Plump and gregarious, these little birds of the homestead flourish on well-attended farm-land, and hold the same place in English hearts as the California quail and Bob-white of the eastern states hold in American hearts. The call of the partridge when the covey assembles at twilight on the harvest field is one of the familiar sounds of the English country-side, a plaintive far-carrying call, a "lights-out" as the birds settle for the night in their family circle in the open field.

The common pheasant has its distinction, too: it is Britain's most beautiful game bird, and probably was introduced into England by the Romans. But compared with partridge or grouse the meat is dry, even tasteless. Of all game birds the pheasant not only can be kept longest but if you would flavor the meat, it *must* be kept. To correct its natural dryness, the bird, on being made ready for the oven, must be dressed with a tightly-fitting waist-coat of bacon fat, and basted abundantly while roasting.

"Hares and Rabbits," or at least "Rabbits." If those are your very first words uttered on the first morning of every month, you will be sure of good luck the month through. So says an old-time superstition. As a child, I tried hard to honor it, repeating the words over and over as I fell asleep the night before in an effort not to miss the chance next morning to ensure my fortune for the month ahead.

The equally old saw, "Catch your hare before you cook it," is attributed to Mrs. Glasse. Her book, *The Art of Cookery Made Plain and Easy by a Lady*, first published in 1747, went through many editions before it bore the lady's name: Mrs. H. Glasse. However, some careless or facetious reviewer changed her word "case" to "catch." In her day, as in Shakespeare's, to case a hare meant to strip off its skin. This may seem an obvious procedure, but Mrs. Glasse, like most of the authors of the old cook books, was not one to skimp her instructions.

It is, I believe, no longer acceptable to truss a hare with its head and ears erect. But once this was customary, and at our home roast hares and rabbit were served that way, except for the hare's ears, which were removed. Over such niceties it is hard to draw a line. To serve a hare in the way of yesterday was certainly no more barbaric than the centuries-old use of a hare's foot as a toilet brush for powder and rouge, a custom that theater folk still favor.

But in whatever way the hare is trussed, he must be very well roasted, and a sprinkling of flour with the last bastings will provide a fine, crisp crust over the meat. Roast hare should be served with a tureen of hot gravy, and red-currant jelly.

Jugged hare is the only proper destiny for an old hare, though even for this ancient dish a young hare is preferable. Either roast or jugged, old or young, hare makes a strong-flavored noble dish.

English rabbits have become rarities because of disease and being harried out as pests. I recall them as part and parcel of our country scene as they came out to feed at the edge of the wood and along the hedgerows on spring and summer evenings. The White Rabbit, and Beatrix Potter's Peter Cottontail and Benjamin Bunny were memorable characters of my nursery books. Their wild cousins provided countless generations of country boys and men with a regular, casual sport of walking round the fields with a gun under the arm on the chance of potting a rabbit for dinner, and of course rabbits were the easiest of all the poacher's quarries. If there had been an English Daniel Boone, I am sure that he would have worn a rabbit-skin cap. Many a time as a small child, I remember creeping along in the shadow of my elder brother, and lying flat down on the ground as he took his aim at a rabbit, my hands in my ears to deaden the bang of his gun. He never, I think, saw me do this: it would have been shockingly unsporting. When it was all over I would, as a golfer's caddy, carry a couple of rabbits for him, proud to be so privileged.

Wild young rabbits' meat is as tender and white as chicken. Roasted like chicken and brought to the table whole, complete with the head, they were served with green peas and new potatoes. We considered the head a delicacy; the meat from the cheek bones was excellent alone, and the tongue and the brains were relished as a spread on bread.

Few people in England now breed squabs, the offspring of domesticated pigeons, that are usually killed for eating when four weeks old. But when salted meat was a staple of the winter diet, pigeon towers or dovecotes—introduced by the Normans—contained up to 500 pairs of pigeons, and were seen throughout England. The feudal "right of dovecot" which survived until Elizabethan days, allowed only lords of the manor and rectors to maintain them, so prized were the squabs.

Nowadays the wild wood pigeon, or Ring Dove, is their noteworthy successor. Like the rabbit, most farmers regard the wood pigeon with an unfriendly eye, because at harvest time they feast on the ripe cut grain before it has been safely gathered in.

However, when plump on their stolen wheat, evidently the sweeter as well, the wild birds are much like bantam-sized poultry. They may be stuffed and roasted like small chicken, with fat bacon laid over their breasts. They make tasty casseroles, too. But the way to serve them in real triumph is the only way that I knew them as a girl—in wild pigeon pie.

Typically English, pigeon pie was, is, and always will be at its utmost when served cold. It was one of our standbys either for breakfast or luncheon, over which I grow nostalgic in memory. If there is one pie among all pies that I would choose to take with me to exile on a desert island, it would be cold wild pigeon pie—as my mother made it.

Pigeon Pie

Pastry:

6 oz. flour

4 oz. butter (or 2 oz. butter and 2 oz. lard), a pinch of salt, a little water

2 hard-boiled eggs
4 to 6 pigeons
1 small onion
1 bay leaf
salt and pepper
Good, clear stock that will make a firm jelly when cold.

The pigeons should be gently cooked until quite tender, with just enough water to cover the disjointed meat, and seasoned with salt, pepper, a small onion and a bay leaf.

When the meat is cooked, set aside until it is cold.

Then put the pigeons into a deep dish pie-dish.

Add two cold hard-boiled eggs cut into quarters.

Pour in the stock.

Cover with the pastry crust.

Brush the pie crust with the beaten yolk of an egg.

Make a slit with a knife in the center of the pie-crust.

Bake the pie at first in a hot oven to raise the crust.

Then let it bake slowly for about 1 hour.

Mushrooms, half a dozen small ones, are an excellent addition.

At home the scalded pigeon feet were arranged to stick up through the center hole in the pie-crust.

Pigeon pie was always eaten cold.

Rabbit Pie

Rabbit pies were made as above, the rabbits being first disjointed and cooked as the pigeons.

The hard-boiled eggs were omitted.

Rabbit pie was always eaten cold.

Jugged Hare

Tall, fire-proof earthenware stewpots with lids used to be made especially for this dish, but a wide-mouthed jar will substitute. The stewpots resembled tall jugs, or pitchers, hence the name Jugged Hare.

Take the best joints of a hare, and

1 tablespoonful butter

1 shallot or small onion

½ doz. cloves

enough thyme, bay, parsley, marjoram, to make a small bunch

1 lemon

4 cups of good stock—preferably beef stock—or enough to fill the packed stewpot nearly to the top

1 glassful of red wine

salt and pepper

Cut the hare into small joints.

Pepper, and dust with fine oatmeal or flour.

Fry lightly and put them into the deep dish.

Add the seasonings:

the onion with the cloves stuck into it

the lemon cut into six pieces

the herbs tied with a string, and attached to the pot handle, set to dangle down inside the pot like a tea-bag the glass of red wine

Pour in the stock so that it completely covers the well-packed-down contents of the dish.

Cover either with a fitting lid, or with a sheet of waxed paper.

Steam for 2 hours in a saucepan of boiling water.

Note:

1 doz. mushrooms is an excellent addition.

The finished dish should come to the table with a white napkin around it, and should be served with

> red-currant jelly
> string beans
> dry toast
> red wine

He consulted Mr. John W. Lea

9. Sauce for the Goose

SAUCE IS THE MOST IMPORTANT caterer to taste on the gastronome's list, so by all means know your sauces. A good one can make a poor dish passable, a passable one good, and beyond that the heights to which a sauce may ascend depend solely on the sauce-maker's art.

The Normans brought sauces to England as a master-stroke in refining the hearty and perhaps too honest fare of the Saxons—a contribution to English living that certainly tempered the bitter taste of the Saxon defeat. It was the Elizabethans who gave the French word *sausse* an original Anglo-Saxon twist, to mean an impudent retort, and saucebox was coined to denote a "saucy"

fellow, not always in a skirt either, for there was the Prince
Francesco Caraccioli.

The prince was a traveler who insisted on eating abroad only
the food to be found at home, and in that mood indulged in a
saucy remark that has outlived his name in history.

"In England," he said, "there are sixty different religions, and
only one sauce."

The libel has endured—libel, I say, because the English
have given the world some excellent sauces. But like most libels,
this one does carry some semblance of truth to which even the
most rabid Anglophile must confess. As a class, England's cooks
are not the best of sauce-makers, but follow humbly in the footsteps of the French.

Back of that humility, I suspect, is more than a submissive
bow to French superiority. Many of the famous French sauces
were created when perishable foods were without benefit of refrigeration and often needed considerable disguising to make
them edible. The sauces of the great Careme, as now adjudged,
often as not killed the flavor of the meat or fish with which they
were served—one ate the sauce without looking too carefully
beneath it. The Anglo-Saxon preferred, and still does, to be sure
of the solid character of his meat or fish.

Maybe another cause for the so-so nature of some English
sauces is that they sound misguidingly simple to make, and for
that reason are all the easier to spoil under a careless hand. In all
the cook's repertoire there is no other single item in which that
oft-repeated and essential ingredient of the old recipe books, care,
is more essential. Unless the foundation of the sauce is exactly
right, nothing can make the finished product good. But anyone
can make a plain sauce if the directions for making it are im-
plicitly followed, and anyone who can make a plain sauce can
make a more elaborate one.

Sauces are the medium for artistry in the kitchen, the royal
road to culinary fame. As the novelist may win acclaim by creating an infinity of situations about the eighteen basic plots, so

the imaginative saucerer can compound an infinity of sauces from a mere handful of foundation sauces, and become the envy of less versatile members of his growing clan. A drop of this, a trace of that, just the right added touch of pepper or salt or oil or vinegar or spice, may become a mountain of glory in building culinary esteem, for the sauce is the test of true genius hovering over the cookpot. Display it, and the world can be yours.

Thinking back now, I believe that The Hyde cooking owed an overwhelming measure of its distinction to its sauces and gravies. My mother and her sisters excelled as saucerers, not with intent to disguise but to enhance the natural flavor of a dish.

The five classic English sauces about which my old home cookery revolved were apple, mint, bread, onion and horseradish. Of the five, apple sauce is the most popular in the United States, to the point that it too has become a colloquialism though with a meaning opposite to saucy. Americans usually prefer mint jelly to the piquant English mint sauce, and use horseradish only as sauce, I think to their loss. The English prefer the young roots freshly-dug and grated just before serving. Sadly I note too that Americans have little or no knowledge of either bread or onion sauce, two of the old reliables of traditional English country fare.

We served apple sauce—best made from green, sharp apples—unfailingly with pork, goose and duck; mint sauce went with both hot and cold lamb; onion sauce with roast mutton, and snowy piles of horseradish accompanied roast beef. Bread sauce added zest to our roast chicken, pheasant, and partridge. This last sauce is said to be the most typically English of sauces, and is the supreme test of an English cook. When properly made it is truly a crowning touch served hot with birds, and no less good when served cold with cold chicken or game.

The old home kitchen also produced a whole series of sauces built on a foundation white sauce. There was cheese sauce to give a lift to vegetable and other dishes; egg, parsley, or anchovie sauces performed a similar duty for white fish. Caper sauce—capers being the unexpanded flower buds of the Mediterranean caper shrub pickled in vinegar—was *the* sauce for boiled mutton. And mace—the powdered husk of the nutmeg nut—flavored a white sauce which sometimes covered completely the cold-boiled fowls which were occasionally served for a cold Sunday supper in summertime, with salad.

Lastly, of prime importance in this group of sauces, was the gravy. This was no mere colored, flavored hot water, but the rich and savory liquid meat extract from the roasted meat or game; only an open roasting pan, constant basting and dredging, will fully yield such gravy. Though today's self-basting covered pans may save hours of after-cleaning, they fail to give the crisped outer crust to a roast, and rob the meat's liquid extract of its full essence. Our home method for gravy-making is described later.

Salad dressings and mayonnaises are the essential sauce accompaniments for salads. English salad dressings come half-way between the simple French and the elaborate American dressings. In England less chopped herbs are used, mustard is generally added, and malt vinegar is often used in place of wine vinegar. In my old home, as in our neighbors' houses, home-made salad dressings, which kept as well as the processed mayonnaises, came to table in tall spiralled glass bottles with glass stoppers, like miniature decanters. Home-made mayonnaise was mainly reserved for boiled salmon.

Alas, nowadays, that custard, a sweet sauce served with various puddings, should so often have to be so deservedly despised. Only rarely is it made either with the care or the proper ingredients of "the good old days." Few of the packaged custard powders that restaurants and time-pressed housewives now use contain a single speck of egg yolk, which properly is a basic ingredient for custard sauce.

Variable as are home cooks and their sauces, today's great paradox is that Britain's industrial saucerers, pickle and condiment makers are consistently good. It is they who now maintain the best traditions of other days when the most prized sauces were the boasts of only the most favored home kitchens. Thanks to the painstaking care of these modern enterprizers, many of the best of the old-time sauces have become world travelers that are as widely recognized as Hereford steers. No list of the world's finest sauces would be complete that omitted Worcestershire sauce, Peter Harvey's sauce, Escoffier's of London, and the wide range of sauces and relishes that bear the label of Crosse & Blackwell.

To know its origin often makes a sauce more piquant. Some of the more famous of today's bottled masterpieces were first contrived by the mothers or wives of English ship-officers in the hope of making their long months at sea more endurable. The men would return home from the Orient with woeful tales of the monotony of salted seafare and hardtack for weeks on end. The remedy: a sauce.

Mrs. Glasse's *The Art of Cookery*, a kitchen bible of its time, lists no less than twenty English sauces. One is specially recommended for "Captains of Ships," a second is suggested to "be taken to the Indies," and Mrs. Glasse tells how to concoct a ketchup that might "be taken around the world."

Worcestershire Sauce, at times incorrectly called Worcester, is a product of reverse origin. A century or more ago, upon retiring as a governor of Bengal, Sir Marcus Sandys brought a recipe of the now-famous sauce back to England with him. He consulted Mr. John W. Lea and Mr. William Perrins, owners of a chemist shop or drug-store on Broad Street, Worcester, to see if they could not reproduce for him this jolly fine stuff with which Hindu chefs flavored so many dishes. So well did Lea & Perrins follow the recipe that Sir Marcus was delighted to pass about bottles of the new sauce among his friends. A generous host who unfailingly maintained a good table at his country estate, his dinners and luncheons brought further acclaim for the unique sauce, until Lea & Perrins were putting in much of their time compounding it. Eventually they acquired from Sir Marcus his treasured recipe as their exclusive possession.

As Worcestershire Sauce, the discovery was soon known and in demand throughout England as a seasoning for all sorts of fish and meat dishes. Travelers carried bottles of it abroad, and gradually the demand became world-wide. One great merit of the sauce was that it was always uniform in flavor, that it was unaffected by the extremes of either hot or cold climates. Messrs. Lea & Perrins were forced to move from their little chemist shop to larger quarters; later, to open sauce factories in other parts of the world. By the mid-1800's a Lea & Perrins factory in New York was supplying the American market.

Imitators have followed, of course, in the wake of Worcestershire Sauce's triumphant course, and the sauce is now sold under many makers' names. But Lea & Perrins continue to be the sole producers of what their bottle labels proclaim is the Original Worcestershire Sauce, made precisely as it was made some 130 years ago from the secret Hindu recipe.

The story of Harvey's Sauce is as English as John Bull. By 1760, the "Black Dog," the old coaching inn at Bedfont in Middlesex, owned by one Peter Harvey, had earned a fine reputation for its food and wine, and also for a curious thin black seasoning called simply Harvey's Sauce. Many of Peter Harvey's customers tried to learn the secret of how this sauce was made. A Mr. Lazenby even offered to buy the recipe, but Harvey refused to part with it.

Lazenby was a prosperous London grocer, a persistent man, and obtaining Harvey's recipe became his over-riding ambition, one that he realized at last by marrying Peter Harvey's sister, Elizabeth. The recipe of the famous sauce was Harvey's wedding present.

Elizabeth, now the wife of a grocer, started to make the most of that slip of paper. She made Harvey's Sauce in her kitchen and sold it to her friends and her husband's customers. From this beginning in 1776 grew the firm of Elizabeth Lazenby & Son Limited, long one of England's premier sauce-makers. And though the company has since been absorbed into another great food concern, the name of Lazenby is still an English household word.

The name of "Escoffier of London" is another evidence that Britons know good sauces when they taste them. French *Monsieur* Auguste Escoffier learned his cooking in the kitchen of his father's restaurant at Nice, and practiced it so successfully at the Petit Moulin Rouge in Paris, that by 1870, when he was 23 years old, his reputation as a chef was established. When the Savoy was opened in the Strand, and M. Ritz began introducing smart Londoners to the Continental habit of supper after the theater, Escoffier was employed as chef. Soon he was an outstanding figure in the London of the 'Nineties, and moved from the Savoy to the Ritz, and then to the Carlton, each move enhancing his culinary fame.

The great dessert *Peches Melba* has nothing to do with sauces, but it has everything to do with Escoffier. While the singer was a guest at the hotel, so the story goes, she asked Escoffier if he could combine in perfect trinity the flavors of vanilla, the peach and the raspberry. The result was his creation, Peaches Melba. But Escoffier's fame rests above all on his sauces. In 1898 he formed the firm of Escoffier, Limited, which he built around sauces. At that time he was chef of the Carlton, and supplying his creations to the British Royal Household, the German Emperor, the Czar of Russia, the House of Commons, as well as to many shipping companies and top-class hotels in England and on the Continent. Escoffier, Limited, was soon exporting to every part of the globe, with the famed chef's sauces winning new royal endorsements wherever they went.

Designed mainly to please English palates, Escoffier's sauces are entirely contrary in conception to those of Careme and most other great French saucerers. He believed in utmost simplicity, and wanted his sauces to enhance and not hide the flavor of the dish with which they were served. He introduced the *essence* foundations—"the evaporated stock obtained by allowing the water, milk or wine in which meat, fish or vegetables happen to be cooked, to steam away slowly so as to leave behind a fragrant concentrate as a basis for whatever sauce will be served with them." *

Among the scores of food items listed today by Escoffier of London are his bottled sauces, chutneys, pastes and relishes, all cast along simple lines. His *Sauce Diable a la Provencale* is the most popular Escoffier sauce in the United States, an extremely piquant accompaniment of all kinds of grill. In England, the most popular is probably his Sauce Robert, a rich and excellently flavored relish for meat, poultry or fish.

Cookery books describe Sauce Robert as one of the simplest, oldest, and most famous of all the French sauces; it was already old when it was listed in a French culinary classic of 1370, and the Normans, its probable originators, also probably brought Sauce Robert to England. The name "Robert" is supposed to be derived from Roebuck Sauce, a favorite accompaniment of venison.

Almost invariably onions are given as the chief basic ingredient of this ancient brown sauce, but Escoffier's version calls for a tomato basis. Escoffier says:

> "It is the late founder's first and probably greatest achievement in table condiments. It has a pronounced, though delicate, flavour peculiar to itself, and forms an excellent addition to chops, steaks and cold meats of every description. When served with venison, hare, pheasant, partridge and other game, it is recommended that Sauce Robert be warmed, have added to it an equal quantity of fresh cream and the whole brought to the boil for two minutes and sent directly to table."

In yet another respect Escoffier added his genius to tradition. His own list of sauces, pickles and chutneys, French mustard and salad dressings, as well as fifteen varieties of fish and meat pates, echoes a note in Mrs. Glasse's cookery book, when she had in mind the monotonous diet of "Captains of Ships," and devised relishes that could "be taken round the world." But Escoffier

* Andre L. Simon, *Guide to Good Food and Wines*, 1956.

went much farther than Mrs. Glasse, and not only had in mind the captains of ships, but the crews and passengers as well.

As a young man he had charge of the headquarters kitchen of the Army of the Rhine during the Franco-Prussian War. He was also a prisoner of war. So he knew first-hand that old maxim that a man cannot fight on an empty stomach, and as a master chef he knew that monotony could be an enemy of appetite. Later, in London, Escoffier accepted an engagement by the Cunard Line to travel in its ships and make recommendations for the cuisine, and the Western Ocean trade has now been carrying Escoffier products for well over a half-century.

Mustard makers and saucerers are running mates. As early as the fifteenth century the French Company of Sauciers joined forces with the *Vinagriers-Moutardiers* and so began a compatible union that later expanded to mustard and sauce makers both in England and the United States of America.

In mediaeval England the mustard seeds were sold to be mixed with honey or vinegar to keep until wanted. About 1720, a Mrs. Clements of Durham had the brilliant idea—it seems so simple now—of grinding the seeds in a mill, and sifting the flour from the husk. Her "Durham Mustard" met with the royal favor of King George I, and rapidly became a nationally popular condiment, which it has remained ever since.

Long before Mrs. Clements, the versatility of mustard as a rough and ready home remedy was securely established, its fame going back to the ancient Greeks. Mustard plasters for colds, bronchitis and neuralgia, and mustard baths as stimulants and an aid to throwing off the common cold helped nurse kings and ploughboys alike back to vigor—no remedy was more widely venerated by our ancestors. One of my earliest recollections of Ladye Grove was a soaking wet day when I had been out shooting with my father and came back looking, probably, like a bedraggled water spaniel. On Aunt Mary's orders I was promptly stripped of my clothes while the old hip bath was brought down from the attic and put in front of the kitchen range. The ancient tin tub—painted appropriately a mustard brown—was filled with water from steaming kettles, and a goodly dose of mustard added. Thereupon, like a scared puppy, I was introduced to the bath that was the cure-all for threatened chills and fever. It was a long time before I had any taste for mustard as it seemed to have penetrated to my innermost soul.

Two of the greatest names among the *Sauciers-Moutardiers* of England are Colman and Keen, and one of the most familiar labels in the English-speaking world is the yellow label on Colman's mustard tins. Keen's name, like Mrs. Clements's, is mostly forgotten, but his firm played a stellar part in the early days of the mustard empire that Colman founded.

Jeremiah Colman was 27 years old when, after serving his apprenticeship, he set up as a flour miller in a windmill at Norwich. Soon he took over a second windmill where mustard as well as flour was milled, and mustard became his main concern. He had no sons, but he did have eleven nephews, who played together as a cricket team. Nephew James Colman was taken into partnership, and Jeremiah sent two other nephews to London to open an office there in 1831.

So prosperous became the business that just after the turn of the century, the Colmans made their first of a series of amalgamations. They took over the famous house of Keen & Sons, at Garlick Mill in the City of London, where Keen's had been making mustard since 1742. Keen's was then the oldest manufacturing business within London city, and operated under the trademark of a scallop shell. The trademark was of double significance, for Keen's offices were hard by the the church of St. James, where St. James's own emblem, the scallop shell, adorned the church porch. Moreover, for as long as men could remember scallop shells had been in general use in grocers' shops for shoveling out mustard and other spices from their bins.

Colman's kept right on growing. The name became so synonymous with dry mustard that Colman's mustard became widely known as English mustard, which Englishmen to this day still prefer to the ready-prepared spiced and seasoned French mustards of the famous *moutardiers* of Dijon.

In America, the dry mustard—Colman's, of course—was as generally used as in England, until in the 1880's along came a spice trader by the name of Robert T. French. He set up the firm of R. T. French Company of Rochester, N.Y., and began to produce French's dry or English mustard. The American housewife who asked merely for English mustard was as likely to get French's mustard as Colman's, which was a bit confusing.

Two sons, George and Francis French, inherited the company upon its founder's death, and Francis proved to be an astute salesman and mixer of French mustard, that is, the true mustard of France. He compounded a new French-prepared mustard to fit the family's name of French, and at once ended the past confusion over names. The buyer who asked for the mustard of France, after 1904, got the French company's version of French mustard—a savory mixture of mustard, vinegar, salt, spices, flavorings, and turmeric.

French mustard, as made by French, soon swept into American leadership. Housewives who in mixing the dry English mustard with water often got a mix that raised the hair, discovered in Mr. French's French mustard a mix that was both safe and tasty. It came in nice glass jars ready for use and so saved work in the kitchen. Besides, Mr. French's mustard, which is really a mustard sauce, may be used on more kinds of food than the peppery dry mustard of Colman's.

Today, throughout America's Old South and Southwest, French mustard by French is preferred by nine persons out of ten, though one of every two New Yorkers and New Englanders still prefers English mustard. Nationally, the favorite is strongly French.

Yet, surprisingly, the ultimate triumph has been Colman's. While the Messrs. French were sweeping forward in the United States of America, back in England the masters of Colman's quietly persisted in pursuing old Jeremiah's policy of amalgamating with worthy rivals, and surely the R. T. French Company was such. Colman's bided their time.

They joined forces with Reckitt & Sons, another old family business that was to starch what they were to dry mustard, and in 1921 the two concerns pooled their overseas trade. This was by way of fortifying the joint arsenal. When, in 1926, George and Francis French, having no male heirs, began looking about for reliable new hands to carry on their business, those of Colman were open and waiting. Old Jeremiah's ghost must have smiled as Colman's English mustard became the guiding brother of French's French mustard. In due course, Reckitt & Colman, Ltd. emerged as the owner of the one and only stock certificate outstanding in the R. T. French Company. That is to say, if you look behind the mustard jar labels of French, America's premier French mustard, you will discover the English name of Colman.

Colman's union with French could not have come at a more opportune time. The hot wiener or frankfurter in a bun—the Hot Dog or American version of the English banger—had become a symbol of American life. And at least one of every two eaters of Hot Dogs preferred them with a smear of French's French mustard.

At home in England, Colman's English mustard mixed with water to just the pepperish degree that you wish is still by long odds the choice. The popularity of dry mustard may even be mentioned in the same breath with the popularity of curry dishes. With these, as with Worcestershire sauce, it was the long arm of British Empire that introduced them to the home table, from India, long enough ago to make them revered traditionals of British fare.

Any English cook will tell you that a curry powder is a ground-up mixture of spices, such as coriander, cloves and cumin, chillies and caraway seeds, mustard, ginger, cloves and pepper. The pungency of the powder and the sauce made from it naturally varies from hot to mild, and in flavor, according to the choices of the mixer. In the old days, when each cook ground and

mixed to his or her own taste and purpose, the curry powders
and sauces were as numerous as the sands, but few people now
grind and mix their own, leaving that chore—and art—to the great
condiment houses. They lean to mildness in their curry sauces,
and to a most commendable consistency.

The name "curry" encompasses a variety of dishes seasoned
with curry sauce. The original Hindu sauce, however, was intended as a relish for rice, the staple diet of the Orient. Britons,
and Europeans too, expanded the uses to many other dishes besides rice: curried chicken, beef, mutton, shell-fish such as shrimps
and prawns, salt-water fish, and eggs—but rice remains the chief
ally to all curried dishes, in the same way that English mustard
prepared to one's individual taste is traditionally the ally of the
Roast Beef of Old England, and as French's French mustard, alias
Colman's, is the ally of at least four billion American Hot Dogs,
half of the annual consumption.

Bread Sauce

½ *pint of milk*
1 small onion
1 leaf of mace
2 oz. stale breadcrumbs
1 clove
1 tablespoonful cream
salt and pepper to taste
¼ *oz. butter*
(the cream is optional, but does improve the sauce)

> The secrets of this sauce are in the use of a double boiler;
> frequent beating during the making, and the addition of
> half the butter before the sauce is removed from the heat.
> Boil the onion for five minutes.
> Pour milk into a saucepan.
> Add the boiled onion, cut into pieces; the mace and the clove.
> Heat slowly and bring to scalding point.
> Remove the mace.

Sprinkle in the breadcrumbs, stirring all the time.
Add salt and pepper to taste, and half the butter.
Cook for about 20 minutes, beating frequently.
Add the cream and the rest of the butter.
Remove the onion and the clove.
And serve immediately.
Bread sauce is excellent with birds. Cold bread sauce is
served with cold roast chicken.

Mint Sauce

3 tablespoonfuls freshly chopped mint
¼ pint vinegar
1 tablespoonful soft sugar melted in ¼ pint of boiling water

When cold, mix the vinegar into the sugared water, adding
the mint last.
Mint sauce is better for "standing" some time before being
served.

Brown Meat Gravy

The basting of meat and game was the all-important prelude
—the first step—in good gravy making. When the roast is
lifted out, sprinkle flour into the fat with a dredger, the
flour being stirred into the meat juices until the mixture
becomes light brown and the juices are all absorbed in the
flour. Stir all the time to prevent burning.
Add salt and a little hot water, stirring until the mixture boils.
This helps to test the "thickness," and if not thick enough,
more flour may be sprinkled in and stirred again to ensure
there are no lumps.
The gravy should be boiled a good minute before being
strained.

White Foundation Sauce

1 oz. butter
1 oz. flour
*11 liquid ounces which may be all milk: or half milk and half
white meat or fish stock*

Set the liquid to simmer for about 15 minutes, flavored according to taste with a bay leaf, a small sprig each of parsley and thyme, a small slice of onion and celery. The lid should be kept on.

Strain the liquid, but keep it hot.

Melt the butter in a small saucepan, over low heat, and do not allow it to sizzle.

When melted, gradually add the flour, stirring it well, and working it, preferably with a wooden spoon, until the mixture is absolutely smooth.

This "roux" (which is its culinary term) should cook slowly, and long enough to cook the flour without boiling it. As soon as the mixture shows signs of bubbling gently, draw the pan from the heat before the mixture colors.

Add the milk, or whatever liquid is being used. The liquid must be added a little at a time, stirred and beaten until the sauce is thick and creamy, but entirely free of lumps. The pan should then be put back over the heat, the mixture stirred until it boils, then it should be allowed to boil 5 minutes.

Season with salt and cayenne, and squeeze in a little lemon juice.

Stir in a bit of butter about the size of a nut, but the sauce must not be allowed to boil after the butter has been added.

Cayenne pepper should be used because it is the only pepper which dissolves and keeps the sauce white. White or black pepper will grey it.

To enrich this plain foundation, add the beaten yolk of an egg, but the sauce should not boil after the yolk has been added.

Brown Foundation Sauce

The method is the same as for the White Sauce up to the point of moving the pan from the fire to prevent the "roux" coloring. The "roux" should be allowed to cook—care taken, of course, not to burn it—until it turns a light coffee color. This may take 20 minutes or longer. Then, instead of adding milk or a milk mixture, add white or brown stock, or water and meat essence, according to the sauce being made.

Equal quantities of butter and flour are used for a general sauce, but if a thin sauce is required, the proportions should be approximately 1 oz. of flour to 2 oz. of butter.

Parsley Sauce

This is simply chopped parsley leaves added to a plain Foundation White Sauce.

Only the leaves and not the stems of parsley should be used, as the stems will color the sauce green.

The sauce must not boil after the parsley has been added.

Egg Sauce

Simply the addition of two or more hard boiled eggs, each cut into 8 pieces, to a plain Foundation White Sauce.

Anchovy Sauce

This English sauce is usually made by adding a little Anchovy Essence to a white foundation sauce in the proportion of

1 teaspoonful of essence to a 1 oz. butter proportioned sauce.

No salt should be added, only pepper, since the anchovy essence is salt enough.

The alternative—the best but most troublesome—method is to pound a couple of de-salted anchovies to a paste, and then rub through a sieve.

Caper Sauce

1 dessertspoonful of capers
½ pint of Foundation White Sauce

The sauce should be made of half milk and half liquor in which the meat is cooked.

Season with salt and pepper, and add the capers, chopped or halved, and serve at once.

The sauce should not boil after the capers have been added.

Onion Sauce

3 large onions
½ pint of Foundation White Sauce

> The sauce should be made of half milk and half white stock.
> Peel and slice the onions, put them in boiling water and cook
>   until tender, and the water boiled up.
> Drain well, and stir them into the foundation sauce.
> Heat through, and serve.
> A little cream is an improvement.

Cheese Sauce

1 oz. butter
1 oz. flour
1 pint milk
6 oz. grated cheese (Cheddar)
¼ level teaspoonful salt
a few grains cayenne pepper
1 teaspoonful made English mustard

> Melt the butter in a saucepan, stir in the flour and cook
>   gently, stirring for 1 minute. Add the liquid a little at a
>   time, stirring well. Bring to the boil, and boil for a minute,
>   stirring. Add the grated Cheddar cheese and seasonings,
>   and stir over gentle heat until the cheese has all melted.

Salad Dressing

Beat up 1 egg
Add: 2 tablespoons cream
*   2 teaspoonfuls sugar*
*   1 teaspoonful mustard (made English mustard)*
*   1 teacup of vinegar*
*   ½ teaspoonful salt*

> Mix thoroughly, and warm over the fire until the mixture
>   thickens.
> Bottle when cold. This dressing will keep for weeks.

Mayonnaise Sauce

Stir a little salt into the yolks of 2 raw eggs.

Add 1½ tablespoons of best salad oil. It is important to stir this in drop by drop, very gradually, and this may take about 20 minutes, stirring to become thick and smooth.

Add ½ teaspoonful tarragon vinegar.

Custard

The word "custard" once represented a kind of open pie, and comes from the old word "crustade," and in French, "croustade" to encrust. Nowadays it covers a much abused sweet sauce. Simplicity itself to make, it is utterly hopeless if not well made.

½ pint of milk
2 well-beaten egg yolks
sugar to taste

Heat the milk in a saucepan.

Add the sugar.

Slowly add the sweetened hot milk to the beaten eggs in the top of a double boiler, and stir slowly until the mixture thickens.

Flavorings, such as vanilla, may be added. An old English favorite flavoring for custard is a bay leaf.

The kitchen garden

10. The Kitchen Garden

WHEN WALTER PAGE SERVED as American Ambassador to Britain in World War I, he made an observation on English vegetables that has taken its place beside Prince Francesco Caraccioli's time-lasting comment on English sauces. There are only three vegetables in England, Mr. Page complained, and two of them are cabbage.

He spoke in war-time, and his remark did convey a half-truth that held all through the lean years. English gardeners can, and do, grow a wide variety of vegetables superbly well, but the average English cook could claim no comparable excellence in conveying the products of their gardens to the table—until very recently.

Far too many hotels and restaurants served cabbage with regular monotony in company with the perennial potato. Worse, the run of cooks presented their vegetables unadorned and badly cooked.

> No other nation treats vegetables quite so casually as the English do... No other nation makes a "melted butter" sauce out of flour and water and pours it over an unfortunate half-drowned cauliflower or vegetable marrow, with the optimistic object of invigorating it.*

* Mrs. C. F. Leyel and Miss Olga Hartley, *The Gentle Art of Cookery*, 1925.

So did English cookbooks of the last 25 years frequently admonish the cooks, and at school, and later through World War II, I would have wholeheartedly agreed both with Walter Page and the author just quoted. But never at home, and certainly not today. Good English restaurants now serve a variety of vegetables of which Walter Page never dreamed, and there is no longer any cause to quarrel with the cooks. They have, now that stringency has lost its grip, reverted to the time-tested traditions of their forebears.

The country gardens of shrubs, flowers and lawns wherein I played during my childhood would have been considered poor affairs, even by us children, if they had not reserved a choice place for the kitchen garden, for fruit and nut trees, cold frames, the seakale pots, the potting shed, and the tall bundles of twiggy sticks ready for staking the great rows of sweet peas along the broad kitchen garden path. Such old-time kitchen gardens served as the outdoor larder, provided fresh fruit and vegetables all through the year, with an abundant surplus for the winter in the form of pickles and preserves.

Our old home's garden was enclosed on three sides by a tall red-brick wall along which much of the fruit was grown, bordered with flowers and herbs, and hedged midway by cordoned apples and pears. There was a "fruit cage" where the soft fruit such as strawberries, red and white and black currants, gooseberries and raspberries were cultivated; when the fruit ripened, a net was thrown over supporting posts to keep out the birds.

The vegetables we grew make a long list—in rebuttal to Walter Page's sighing generalization. Though a few standbys of the American kitchen garden were missing—neither corn nor lima beans do well in the cool English summer—we grew other vegetables that Americans know only slightly, if at all.

We had several varieties of French beans; broad and runner beans; early, maincrop, and late peas. There were early and long-keeping carrots, leeks and celery, beetroot and spinach, potatoes and parsnips and turnips—England grew and used these last in

place of potatoes long before potatoes reached Europe from South
America via Spain. We had the Globe and Jerusalem artichokes,
an asparagus bed, and in a row of massive earthenware pots, with
little lids atop, the seakale was forced to an early edibility.

Seakale is a native plant of most sea coasts of Western Europe,
and is grown for its leaf-stalks. These are bleached and forced in
the protective pots so as to be ready to eat in late winter and
early spring. Then we would lift the lids and peer into the big
pots' dark interior, and if the frail white stalks were "ripe" we
reached down and cut them off carefully with a sharp knife. Simmered until tender, and served with melted butter or a very light
white sauce, seakale is no mean delicacy.

The main crop onions served three purposes: first, as spring
scullions; secondly, after being thinned out, and grown into
proper little onion bulbs, they were used for pickling; lastly, those
left were encouraged to mature into the large size six-month
"keeping" onions for winter storage. We thought the shallot, a
diminutive member of the onion tribe, indispensable. This is a
small underground bulb onion, easier and more reliable to grow,
milder in flavor than the onion proper, and it makes an excellent
flavoring for soups and stews. Shallots mature by midsummer,
fully three months before the maincrop onions are harvested:
two-by-three-inch firm, tender bulbs, in shiny coppery-yellow
skins. They are worthy successors of the early spring scullions,
and take their place over a long period as the countryman's
favorite relish with his bread, cheese and beer.

We grew the usual saladings; lettuces in succession, tomatoes,
cucumbers. The English cucumber, grown in heated houses or
frames, is longer and more slender than the ridge cucumbers that
are grown out-of-doors without protection. The vegetable marrow
is *the* member of the great race of marrows, squashes and gourds,
and English gardeners grow it in preference to all others. Green
or yellow, sometimes round but usually thick and long, vegetable
marrows are, to my mind, invariably insipid when boiled, but

they are delicious when stuffed young, and also, when old and tough, made into a very English preserve, marrow jam.

Among the ill-treated cabbages, we grew spring cabbage, savoys, sprouting broccoli, and curly leafed kale; cauliflowers and red cabbage—mostly for pickling—and that autumn bastion and favorite accompaniment of roast pheasant and roast beef, the Brussels sprouts, which are a British speciality despite their name. And it is worth remembering that although the homely cabbage has been, and will probably continue to be ruined by many cooks, when properly treated it is the most important of all vegetables dietetically. The Romans venerated the cabbage as an antidote for drunkenness, and as being good for the eyes, the digestion, pains in the back, gout, ulcers, chilblains, sciatica and wounds —even snake bites.

An inventory of our summer meals would read like an eight-eenth-century year book, for our home-grown fruits and vege-tables rang the changes as the weeks went by. And there was nothing casual in our kitchen treatment of them. A cauliflower casserole prepared with cream and grated cheese covering the briefly cooked and separated young flowerlets, and served with salad, was a meal in itself. A young marrow, cooked whole and stuffed with a savoury filling of finely chopped pork or beef and dusted with thyme, sage, chives, tarragon, mint and parsley, was truly a gardener's reward. Buttered new potatoes never came to table without a sprinkling of finely chopped parsley over them. Peas were never cooked without a sprig of mint; this is an en-tirely English culinary practice that greatly enhances the peas, however young and tender they may be.

A dish of young peas, picked and shelled a half hour before being slipped into the boiling water with the mint, is an English gardener's pride and joy. For nowhere in the world can peas be grown so perfectly as in the gentle rain-washed English spring and early summer, and for most gardeners nothing is so prideful as the picking of his own peas after a day of soundless, misting, pea-swelling rain.

And so it was with all the vegetables we grew, with all the fruit that ripened on our mellowed brick walls, with the game we shot, the fish we caught. They were very much a part of the leisured life of the old, comely England before the time-saving methods of the tin can era pushed them so abruptly into the past. Everything we ate had overtones and memories. We knew all about our food from A to Z, as the craftsman knows everything about the wood he fashions—its age, its grain, its habit under the chisel and later under the finisher's brush.

Knowing when to gather vegetables from the garden is just as important as using care, instead of casualness, in cooking them. The "when" may be remembered by contrasting the harvesting of vegetables with fruit. Fruit is hard in youth, usually must be gathered when of mature age and fully ripe. Vegetables are tender in youth and must be gathered while they are still young, except for some of the winter-keeping root vegetables. So the good gardener tries to preserve in his vegetable garden that fleeting tender quality which belongs to youth alone, and cannot be bought. If he keeps his produce until it is past its flush of youth he is no better than the truck gardener who, for the sake of profits, must grow for size, and weight, and shipping quality.

In spite of the tin can, England today is one of the last great strongholds of home-grown vegetables. It is a nation of gardeners who devote as much time to growing vegetables as flowers, and who probably eat more fresh vegetables than any other of the English-speaking peoples. In the kindly, temperate climate, amateur gardeners routinely and lovingly supply their households with a variety of fresh vegetables the year round—to the tune of nine per cent of all the food consumed, worth about one hundred million pounds sterling a year. The city housewife is, of course, less lucky. For her, vegetables are the supreme example of the tag: what you gain on the roundabouts you lose upon the swings. She can save time and work and perhaps money by buying the standard products of the food factory, but she pays in her loss of flavor and freshness which are the joys without price won by harvesting your own.

Three standbys among English vegetables, the Jerusalem artichoke, the Scarlet Runner and Broad beans, rarely appear in American food markets, though they are listed in United States seed catalogs, and two of them hailed originally from the Americas.

The Jerusalem artichoke, which is neither an artichoke nor has any connection whatsoever with the Holy Land, was introduced into Europe by the French explorer, Champlain, who first noticed it as a cultivated plant in Massachusetts in 1605. The French originally called the artichokes *pommes de terre,* for they resemble potatoes more than anything else. But the knobbly tubers or roots are easier to grow, flourish in poor or rich soil alike, are immune from pests, and keep well for months. The name Jerusalem supposedly became attached to them as a result of Europeans wrestling with the Indian tribal name of *Topinambour.* Probably somebody, in despair, cried "Oh, Jerusalem!" and that was it.

This winter vegetable is wrongly considered time-consuming to prepare. Jerusalem artichokes should not be peeled or pared but should be washed and well scrubbed only; the skins are rubbed off the irregular surface after boiling or steaming. The tubers should be served with a coating of melted butter or with a white sauce. Best of all, in the opinion of many, they provide a delicious thick white soup.

The spectacular Scarlet Runner bean is to England what the pole and lima beans are to America. Introduced into Europe from Mexico in 1633, it has long been a favorite of English gardeners. At first the old reliable runner was grown only as an ornamental plant, and not until the eighteenth century was its food value recognized; plant breeders then got busy and improved the length and quality of the pods. Today's best garden varieties bear pods up to twenty inches long. Customarily they are shredded and sliced before cooking, a practice that gourmets decry because of the resulting loss, so they say, of both flavor and vitamins. At home we had them young, sliced, and relished them as an accompaniment to roast beef.

In the United States, the Runner Bean is still grown as it was first grown in England. Seed catalogs list it among the ornamental vines, as bearing large showy stems of bright scarlet flowers, but they do note that the bean is edible too. (In California the plant is a disappointment from the English point of view: the climate is too hot.)

Respect should be paid the Broad bean or *Faba vulgaris,* the common bean, as it is known to botanists, as the oldest cultivated bean of history. The English have grown it probably since the Roman occupation. Yet too many gardeners pick the pods beyond their prime, and that fault and careless cooks together are responsible too often for the ancient bean's abuse. In America, it is little known and often is confused with and called by the name of its field variety, the horse bean, *Faba equina,* which is grown as fodder for cattle and horses. The true Broad bean is only listed briefly in a few American seed catalogs, and appears but occasionally in the food markets that serve Italian communities. The Italians, however, know their beans, and I have seen the Broad bean growing in their backyards in San Francisco—with good reason.

Flat, broader than any other bean, more nutritious than wheat, the Broad bean is even older than history as a prized food of man. It was cultivated by the lake-dwellers of Switzerland and northern Italy, in Egypt, and long before the Christian era in China, Japan and India. Thus the history and survival of the Broad bean parellels that of corn (maize, or Indian corn, as it is called in England) which the American Indian cultivated long before the arrival of Columbus, and is considered one of the Red Man's greatest gifts to the white man. Neither the Broad bean nor corn have any means of dispersing themselves by their seeds; except for their cultivation and development by man, they would have been lost centuries ago in the struggle for existence.

Vegetable growing was a great art with the Romans, and though the Saxons grew vegetables before the Roman Occupation, the Romans introduced many more, and might be called the fathers of the English kitchen garden. Many of the botanical names of European vegetables are derived from the surnames of the landed Roman proprietors who were responsible for growing them. The Pisones gave their name to Pisum, the Pea; the Lentulus, to the Lentil, and the Fabii to Faba, the Bean. And if the Roman, Horace, was not the first to discover it, he was the first to set down his liking of the now classic combination of a dish of beans joined with a rasher of bacon.

The Broad bean was the only vegetable known as a bean in Europe up to the sixteenth century, when other vegetables introduced from South America and the Orient, such as the Scarlet Runner Bean, were also called beans.

To know the true worth of the Broad bean you must be your own gardener. Then pick your beans when youth is still surging through them, and cherish them in the cooking. Do that, and your dish of beans will equal one of fresh green peas. What is true of all non-root vegetables applies more to the Broad bean than to any other vegetable the gardener grows. The essential quality of youth cannot be bought, or passed by when it is ready at hand.

Broad beans are at their best when gathered young and tender, cooked speedily, and served with a pat of butter. At their second best, or in the first flush of middle age, they require longer cooking, and may be served with parsley sauce. Do not judge them by what you see in the market place, where they are invariably too old, and encased in leathery tough skins within their furry-lined pods. The only remedy at this stage is to remove the skins by throwing the beans in fast-boiling water and blanching them. Superior in flavor to the lima bean, Broad beans are excellent served with parsley sauce and boiled fowl and boiled ham. They are, as Horace said, the perfect accompaniment of bacon, or bacon and eggs. They may also be served cold as garnishings for soups and salads.

It is good garden practice to top the plants when the pods have set. This removes the black fly which loves to cluster atop the plants, and also helps the pods to grow. Moreover, the gathered tops are like the tenderest spinach, and equally as good as the prized "bean sprouts" of the Chinese.

Lastly, the Broad bean has one quality that no other vegetable possesses, and not all flowers either. Its blossoms yield an exquisite perfume, which the perfumers have distilled into a natural flower scent that ranks with the jasmin and the rose. Associations bound up with scents are notoriously vivid: the scent of baking bread may recall a certain stone-flagged, raftered kitchen; for an Italian-American the scent of his *Faba* may stir memories of northern Italy. For an Englishman, the scent of beanfields after rain is as poignant as the sight of the first primrose of spring, or a wheatfield at harvest time.

She made Harvey's sauce

Jerusalem Artichokes   Boiled.

Artichokes should be washed and scrubbed, not peeled nor pared.

They should be steamed or boiled with just enough water to cover them, and the water should be saved as it sets to a firm jelly and is an excellent basis for soups.

When tender, rub off skins, and finish in butter in oven, or serve with a white sauce.

Jerusalem Artichoke Chips

Parboil and rub off the skins.

Dry well and cut in very thin slices.

Fry in deep fat to a golden brown, and

Serve with a sprinkling of salt and finely chopped parsley over them.

Jerusalem Artichoke Soup

2 lbs. artichokes

1 pint of white stock

1 oz. of butter

2 onions

1 pint of milk

2 tablespoonfuls of cream

1½ oz. flour

¼ teaspoon cayenne

1 blade of mace

salt and pepper

Boil the artichokes. Put them into cold water and reboil.

Strain and make a puree of them.

Boil the mace with the milk.

Have ready a saucepan large enough to hold all the soup.

Melt the butter in the saucepan.

Mix the flour in the butter until it is quite smooth.

Add, slowly, the stock, the milk and seasonings, and lastly, the artichoke puree.

Bring to the boil and serve, with small croutons of fried bread.

The cream should be added only after the soup is taken off the fire.

Stuffed Vegetable Marrow

Cut off the end of the marrow and scoop out the seeds.

Make a filling of: tomatoes, brown breadcrumbs, minced beef or mutton or the endbits off a ham bone. Season with salt and pepper and chopped parsley, and bind with an egg.

The filling must be dry and savoury, since the damp marrow will steam the filling.

Replace the cut-off end and make firm with skewers, and bake, basting well from time to time with butter until the marrow is tender.

To Pickle Onions—and Shallots

Pack the onions into wide-mouthed jars.

Simmer peppercorns in vinegar (1 pint or whatever quantity required) for a short time, and then allow to get quite cold.

Pour cold vinegar over the onions, and tie down the jars.

To Pickle Red Cabbage

Cut the cabbage up into fine shreds. Place the shredded cabbage on a big dish or trays, with layers of salt, and leave for 24 hours.

Next day, shake all salt off the cabbage, and put it into wide-mouthed jars.

Boil 1 pint of vinegar with
    1 teaspoonful of peppercorns
    6 cloves
    1 blade of mace.

Then allow the vinegar to get quite cold.

Pour the cold vinegar over the cabbage, and tie down the jars.

Mustard Pickles or Piccalilli

1 large cauliflower
2 lb. onions
2 lb. cucumbers or gherkins
1 lb. sugar
1 oz. turmeric powder
1 oz. mustard (English)
2 teaspoonfuls of mustard seed
1 teaspoonful of peppercorns
1 tablespoonful cornflour
1 quart vinegar (approx.)

Wash vegetables, breaking the cauliflower and cutting the onions and cucumbers into small pieces. Cover with brine made of salted water and allow to stand 24 hours.

Bring to boil in same solution, then drain thoroughly.

Mix turmeric powder and mustard and cornflour to a smooth paste with a little vinegar and add to a saucepan with the remaining vinegar.

Stir in the vegetables; add the peppercorns and mustard seed tied up in a little muslin bag.

Boil all together gently, stirring frequently, for approximately 40 minutes when the mixture will have thickened.

Remove the muslin bag and pour hot into hot sterilized glass jars.

To Pickle English Walnuts

Pierce the walnuts when they are green and young enough for a big needle (or knitting needle) to pass right through them.

Make a brine to cover them entirely with
      6 oz. salt
      1 quart of water.

Take off the scum which rises to the surface as the salt dissolves.

Throw in the walnuts, well pierced in several places, and stir night and morning. Change the brine every 3 days.

If required at once, the walnuts should remain in the brine for 12 days.

If required to keep, change the brine for 9 days. Then drain the walnuts and spread them on racks or dishes, and let them remain exposed to the air and sun, turning them now and then, until they become blackened. This will take two days or less.

Make a pickle for the nuts with a good ½ gallon measure of vinegar to 100 walnuts.

Add 1 teaspoon of salt
2 oz. of black pepper
3 oz. of bruised ginger root
¼ oz. cloves
a blade or two of mace.

Boil this pickle for 5 minutes. Have the walnuts already in their stone jars, and pour the vinegar on them as it is taken from the fire.

When cold tie down.

If any additional vinegar needs to be added,—the walnuts must be kept entirely covered with the pickle—the added vinegar should first be boiled.

The 9 days brine curing will keep walnuts good for 10 years.

To Pickle Mushrooms   (The wild, field mushroom).

Gather small button mushrooms. Cut the stems quite close off the fresh mushrooms, and clean them gently with a piece of flannel slightly moistened and dipped into fine salt. Throw the mushrooms as they are done into fresh cold water mixed with a large spoonful of salt. When all are cleaned and washed, drain all water from them.

For every quart of mushrooms allow nearly 1 quart of the palest white wine vinegar.

Add: 1 heaped teaspoonful of salt
½ oz. whole white pepper
1 oz. bruised ginger
¼ saltspoon cayenne pepper
2 or 3 small blades of mace.

When the pickle boils, throw in the mushrooms and boil for 6 to 9 minutes. If some mushrooms are larger than the others, put them in and boil them for 2 or 3 minutes before putting in all the rest.

As soon as the mushrooms are tolerably tender put them at once into warm jars or bottles. Pour over the vinegar, and divide the spices evenly in the jars. When cold, tie down securely.

Blackberrying

11. The Fruit Garden

APPLES, PEARS, PLUMS and berried fruits ripen slowly in England, and come to a full-flavored maturity that is unsurpassed in any other climate. It should not be surprising, therefore, that the English long have been expert both in growing and in using fruit: as fresh dessert, in pies and puddings, and in a vast variety of jam and jelly preserves.

Among all fruits, the apple is the Englishman's first choice; no other so accords to the national taste; none has a longer season, lasting in variety with proper keeping through eleven months of the year. June is the only month when the well-managed country home is without apples.

The apple was one of the few trees that the original Britons, the pioneering settlers from mainland Europe, like Johnny Apple-seeds, introduced into Britain centuries before the Roman invasion directed by Julius Caesar. It was the apple that gave the English sidewalk fruit-vendor the name of costermonger, from the time he sold Costard apples in the streets of London in Shakespeare's day—the Costard apple is the oldest English variety on record, dating to 1292. It was an apple tree in fruit that England's Royal Horticultural Society, in 1817, took for its coat of arms. And to the English school-boy no fruit is so worth climbing a fence for as a dangling apple; an English connoisseur of fruit will become more eloquent over the flavor of a prime dessert apple than over any other fruit, judging it with the same loving deliberation as a Frenchman does a fine wine.

Good English cooks make a clear and fine distinction between cooking apples and dessert apples. The cooking apple is among fruits what the potato is among vegetables, being used for an infinity of dishes. Yet by no means are cooking apples regarded as ordinary apples. The late Edward Bunyard, an authority on such matters, said that "the best English apples by long training know how to behave in a pie; they melt but do not squelch; they inform but do not predominate." * He defined the perfect apple for a pie as one that preserves its individuality and form, and does not go to a pale, mealy squash, but becomes soft and golden. "In flavor it must be sharp, or what's the use of your Barbados sugar? It should have some distinct flavor of its own, not merely a general apple flavor." Apples such as Golden Noble, Wellington, Ontario, and the great September-October Bramley, king of cooking apples, all meet these requirements.

Regular English dishes include Apple Charlotte, baked apples and apple dumplings, apple turnover and apple pie, which is the Pie of pies. An English apple pie is quite different from the American, and the difference is not so simple as the definition between pie and tart, namely that a pie is enclosed and a tart exposed. Pie, says the Oxford Dictionary, is "a dish enclosed in or covered with a layer of paste and baked." The statement presupposes that the only apple pie worthy of the name is the English type of apple pie, which is made in a deep crockery pie-dish with top crust only.

I can see Lena, my faithful nurse, who "stayed on" many years as our cook, standing by the kitchen table, rolling the paste, lifting it from the floured board, and rolling it again with the wooden rolling-pin which always seemed her emblem of authority. Year in, year out, her apple pie was made in precisely the same way, and always turned out precisely right.

Our apple pie, as the recipe will show, disdained any pastry

* Edward Bunyard, *The Epicure's Companion*, 1937.

lining in the deep dish. Such a top-crust-only pie has a great advantage over a pie baked in a shallow pie pan with crusts both top and bottom, the lower of which becomes soggy overnight. Too, the deep-dish pie has a more generous portion of fruit, which is luscious when hot and some think even better when eaten cold the next day.

Early cooking apples are not true pie-makers, and in the cook's apple-season calendar, apple pudding leads the pudding and pie parade. This begins formally, with proper flourishes in the kitchen to mark the great event, with St. Swithin's Day, July 15th. Somehow or other the weather-wise old saint was a judge of ripening apples too, for according to age-old English country superstition apples can only be "safely eaten" after the Blessing of the Apples on St. Swithin's Day. Like so many of the old superstitions, this one no doubt had its practical purpose, to ensure against the dire results of children eating hard, green apples.

Both at The Hyde, and in my own home, our unfailing St. Swithin's Day ritual was to have for dinner a boiled apple-pudding with a suet crust. The apples were codlins, and by that time our trees were heavy with the pale early fruit. As far back as in June, our month of apple dearth, I began looking forward to that St. Swithin's Day pudding, and was never disappointed. The pudding was served boiling hot, and when my portion was sliced and placed before me, its fragrance rose with the steam to proclaim the rebirth of our orchards.

As good as that first cooked apple dish was, it never outplaced the fresh eating-apple, or dessert apple. I remember being chided once by a friend when I called a dessert apple simply an eating apple. That, he said, placed all apples in two classes, eaters and cookers. I was reminded that all apples are "eaters," but that only *dessert* apples are eaten uncooked, and merit the distinction of being so called.

Among dessert apples, Cox's Orange Pippin, or Cox's Orange, or simply Cox, reigns supreme. Developed by a retired brewer in 1830, Cox apples carefully graded and packed in boxes make a prize present for any apple gourmet at Christmastime. The apple is acid and sharp in October; at its best in November and December, loses some excellence after January but will keep in a cool cellar until May, a fine apple to the last. "At the end of its season it is just like an old claret. Aroma still there, acid gone, so that the sweetness is a little too marked for some palates; the flesh has now become very tender, but, if properly kept, still full of juice." *

But even Edward Bunyard declared that he who limits himself only to a Cox loses much. The names of other favored dessert apples read like a wine-list: Beauty of Bath, for August; James Grieve and Worcester Pearmain, which come to market in September; Ribston Pippin, in October; Blenheim Orange in October and December; and Orleans Reinette, which runs with the Cox from December to March.

At home, apples were almost always on hand like the daily bread: cooked in one form or another, or eaten fresh as dessert after a confectioned sweet, on elegant plates with their attendant silver-bladed dessert knives and forks, and finger bowls. Many a Sunday in autumn we would walk the six miles to Ladye Grove instead of driving the dog-cart, so that we might go slowly through the orchards testing the flavor of this or that apple against last year's ripening, according to the summer's weather. On these occasions my mother carried a little silver-bladed pocketknife for use in sampling her favorites, such as the old Sam's Crab, and others that now survive only in memory. Best of all, I think, I liked the winter bedtime apple, chosen from the basket of Coxes, Blenheims and Russets that were brought into the house as the last act of the day, and eaten as we sat around the open fire.

From the English cook's viewpoint, the berried fruits are more important than pears or stone fruit, such as peaches, nectarines, and cherries. Few people in England can afford to be profligate with peaches, nectarines or even apricots, since these do not grow as luxuriantly as they do in warmer climates and are, accordingly,

* Edward Bunyard, *The Epicure's Companion*, 1937.

prized and reserved as fresh dessert. Apricots can be an exception. One variety known as Moor Park, introduced a hundred and fifty years ago, ripens in a kind summer on many a Cotswold stone wall, a glorious golden fruit with a characteristic red-brown blush upon it.

Pears can be bottled or "canned" in glass jars after paring and halving for winter use, but are best when taken straight from the tree, next best after being stored with the same care that is given prime dessert apples. Cherries, too, are best gleaned fresh from the tree, though cherry pie is popular enough in cherry growing districts to be honored by its own day, Cherry Pie Sunday, which comes the first week in August.

Plums as a class do not attain the rank of dessert fruits, and are best under the cook's hand in plum pie or puddings, and above all as plum jam. The exception is the gage plum or greengage, which is so superior to the commonplace varieties of the prolific plum family as to be regarded as a plum apart. This distinction, I believe, is wholly British, and arose when a member of the Gage family imported a French plum, Reine Claude, and lost the label. The fruit was re-named to commemorate Mr. Gage's absent-mindedness.

The true greengage is the plum of plums, luscious either for dessert or preserved as greengage jam. There are several varieties, among which my father preferred the Transparent or Old Green-gage. He grew it, as much of our fruit was grown, espaliered on the warm brick walls that enclosed our garden. Old Green-gage ripened in September. We rated it higher than either peach or nectarine, and the first ripe gage was always picked and presented to my mother with ceremony.

The greengage must be eaten when it is dead-ripe, when the fruit has become slightly shrivelled around the stalk, and a flush of red tinges the transparent amber. So you must seek the *perfect* gage in your own or a friend's garden, and never hope to find it marketed. Even when you track it down, a dead-ripe gage is always a gamble, a race between the wasps and you.

Damson plums are also in a class of their own. Small and oval, they are closely related to the tart wild sloes of the hedgerow, when ripe are a black "damson blue" with a green flesh inside. Damsons never figure among dessert fruits because they are passably good only when eaten fully ripe from the tree on a thirsty damson-picking day. But to me they are by far the best and most versatile cooking plum.

"Damn the damsons!" one of my cousins used to say, year by year, when the time came to pick the heavy and commercially rewarding crop. Yet, we were always grateful, kitchen-wise, for a good damson year. No other plum has so many uses: for cordials and pickles, for jam and jelly, pies and puddings; for the wholly British damson cheese, and a compote which the British—I think uniquely—call a fool. This the dictionary defines as a dish of stewed fruit, but that is a gross injustice. A fool is a compote or puree of fruit pulp mixed with either cream or custard, and properly only two fruits, the damson and the gooseberry, are made into fools.

Of course the berried fruits are the first to ripen in the fresh-fruit year, and in England they include strawberries and raspberries; currants, black, white and red, and gooseberries. The strawberry is wholly American in origin, though continental Europe knows it as "the English strawberry" to distinguish it from the alpine varieties with small berries. It is English only by virtue of an English marriage of two American immigrants, one from Virginia and the other from Chile.

From wherever they come, strawberries are best when they come to the table fresh from the garden, and are eaten with cream. And hygienists of this cellophane-wrapped age to the contrary notwithstanding, it is heresy either to cut, peel or wash the berries: such atrocities drain off half the flavor. For the *perfection* of garden-ripened strawberries and cream, you must be willing to risk adding to that peck of dirt which, the proverb says, we all must eat before we die. There is, however, I'll grant, a distinction between the strawberry ripened by the commercial grower in the field, and the strawberry on which the amateur gardener lavishes special care, as every real English gardener does. He fits straw mats around each strawberry plant so that the rain does not splash his ripening fruit with earth.

Strawberries and cream are one of the joys of June: strawberries dropped whole and unwashed into a deep, cold glass dish that is half-full of cream slightly whipped, then stirred in the cream, some of the fruit being bruised or slightly mashed, and allowed to stand an hour. When the cream and the fruit have mingled so that the cream will not cover another single strawberry, dredge white sugar over the pale pink mass, and serve straightaway.

The only rival dish to strawberries with cream is to serve the berries in cups or deep plates, dredge them with sifted sugar, and pour either claret or champagne over the sugared fruit. The wine is antiseptic comfort for those who shun the unwashed berries, and the flavors of wine and berries blend and compliment each other. On the continent the small garden-grown Alpine strawberries are preferred in this fashion.

Much the same may be said of raspberries which in England are red or yellow, rarely black. They seem slightly less in favor than strawberries, partly because they do not "carry" well to market. But with raspberries and cream, it is best to sweeten the whipped cream before adding the fruit. Pour half the sweetened cream into the serving dish, "bruise" the fruit into it, and mix fruit and cream with a seasoning of rosewater. Then add the remainder of the cream before a final stirring of all together, and you will know raspberries well worth knowing.

Between red and white currants the only difference is color, but black currants stand alone. They differ from their red and white cousins as the damson differs from other plums. The black currant is something of an English speciality, and makes a fine and unusual jam as well as cordials and tea, pies and puddings. Black currant pie is ranked by gourmets as one of the best and most typically English of all fruit pies.

The gooseberry was English bred and is at its best in its native climate; it may be round or oval, smooth and downy, or rough and hairy-skinned; red, yellow, green or white when ripe. Some regard it as a plebeian, some complain of its tough skin when eaten fresh from the bush, others declare it as worthy of dessert status as the best tropical fruit. There are gooseberries and gooseberries, and the best of them rank as the greengage ranks among plums.

Gooseberries are gathered in various stages. For dessert or jam they should be ripe, and if for dessert picked in the hottest sun, and eaten when still sun-warmed if possible. They are picked young, green and still hard for such dishes as pies, puddings, fool and meringue, and for bottling for winter use. (To the English cook "bottling" is the household term for the American's "putting up" in glass, though both use the same kind of glass jar.)

Although our garden provided us amply with all sorts of good things, the harvest of the field and hedgerow was valued too. We treasured the wild fruits two-fold; for their excellence as preserves, and because finding and gathering and bringing them home in triumph were among the joys of the country year. Most of our preserves of field and hedge could never be bought but were always home-made.

The bramble, as the wild English blackberry is called, is the sweetest of all blackberries. No cultivated berry can touch it, a fact that has made the bramble one of the few English field fruits that has invaded commerce as well as the home kitchen. A wayside fruit, the wild blackberry in season always gave us the excuse to loiter on a long walk, refreshed us on the way home after a day's fishing, and meant a day's outing for the cook. Blackberrying was an annual expedition of late August or early September when, dressed in our oldest clothes, we set forth armed with white enamel milk-cans instead of baskets, so that none of the precious juice would be lost. We knew that we were in for scratches on hands, arms and legs, but that was a small price to pay for blackberry-and-apple puddings and pies, and "bramble," *the* blackberry jelly without compare.

Hip-and-haw jelly was another prized hedgerow preserve. It is made from the haws of the hawthorn and the hips of the wild rose, which grows everywhere in England. Amber-red, with a warm smokey flavor, to my mind hip-and-haw is far superior to the best apple jelly, whether made from crab apples or enhanced by quince or a scented geranium leaf. Somebody discovered during World War II that the wild rose hips are rich with Vitamin C, and the old-time jelly had a war-time revival which brought long-forgotten recipes back into home kitchens.

Few people bother nowadays with the old-time "home" wines and cordials, but we did with seasonal consistency, and our elder flowers and elder berries, the dandelions and the cowslips never went to waste. The juice pressed from the elder flowers became a clear, sparkling, light summer wine, while a pinch of the dried blossom gave a magical touch to apple pie at any time of the year. The elderberry juice was set aside in our still-room to ripen into a winter wine with the red glow of claret, or with sugar and spice added was cooked down to a syrup, which became a winter cordial to be taken hot as a curative drink for colds. The remedy made a cold almost worth its childhood nuisance.

Elderberry, dandelion and cowslip wines were winter luxuries among our country cottagers, and when well made and kept resembled bottled sunshine. Today, they belong to that other age before anybody dreamed of flying to the moon, before luxuries were strictly things that must be bought.

The freckled yellow flowers of the cowslips found other uses for the mere cost of the gathering. We children picked them atop their long stalks, which we twisted and tied into round, sweet-smelling nosegays that made wonderful play-balls. At home, the cowslip petals garnished Maytide salads. The flowers are still there, free for the gathering, but the play-balls have become rubber, and who today would be so primitive as to offer wild cowslip petals as a golden touch to any meal?

The jam cupboard at my old home contained the result of a monumental amount of work in the home kitchen—perhaps it is better that it also belonged to that "other age." We had our own fruit, lush and ripening, on our own trees; we *knew* that no "store" jam or jelly could be as good as our own home-made products, so we kept clear of the commercial counters and bent willingly to the kitchen toil.

Certain small niceties went with it. For instance, the stones of all stoned fruit were cracked and the kernels added to the jam when cooking; though with apricot jam we used by preference a few split almonds. Like the "family-five" pickles of walnut, mushroom, onion, red cabbage and our own piccalilli, there were the family-five jams: black currant and damson, which we considered the best of all for jam tarts; greengage, the plum of plum jams; commonplace plum, and marrow, or marrow and ginger jam. Black currants were also made into a thick syrup that sweetened with honey was a hot bed-time drink for hoarseness of the throat or to loosen a cold on the chest. And, of course, there was red currant jelly and blackberry jelly.

From among the oldest of English country recipes we made three fruit preserves that may be described as fruit butters in their stiffest form: apple cheese, damson cheese, and lemon cheese or curd. Both apple and damson cheese are at their best after keeping a time, up to a year; they make delicious winter desserts and, too, damson cheese may be served with meat to make a change from red currant jelly.

Of the three old-timers, lemon curd is the best known today in Britain if not to the world outside. It is not exported since it does not keep so well, containing both butter and eggs. It can be made any time of the year, but at my old home February was lemon curd-making month, because then lemons were at their best and eggs were most plentiful. Stored in the cool, dry, dark jam cupboard our curd kept perfectly well until the following December. It makes a rich spread for bread and butter, and for layer cakes, but is most generally used as a tartlet filler for

Lemon Curd Tartlets. The method of making lemon curd is always the same, but the quantities of sugar, eggs, butter and lemons that are used vary like the alternative solutions to a cross-word puzzle. An English paper recently listed the variations as follows:

A	Sugar 8 oz.	Eggs 2.	Butter 3 oz.	Lemons 2.
B	Sugar 5 oz.	Eggs 2.	Butter 5 oz.	Lemons 2.
C	Sugar 8 oz.	Eggs $\frac{2}{3}$	Butter 4 oz.	Lemons 2.
D	Sugar 8 oz.	Eggs 2.	Butter 2 oz.	Lemons 1½.

After which it seems reasonable to ask: Are the old recipes worth the work—why not buy your lemon curd or jam or jelly at the nearest good store?

The answer lies in a second question: Do you love to cook? If you do, nothing that you can buy will taste quite so good as your own creation to which you have added the priceless ingredient of fun. However, aside from fun, the truth is today that Britain's "store" jams and allied products, among which one must include marmalade, are as good as the best the old-home kitchens ever turned out.

Evidence of that fact is the world-wide fame of the great British jam-and-jelly houses such as Coopers of Oxford, Keillers of Dundee, Chivers, and Wilkins of the Tiptree Brand. These firms, indeed, have done the average Englishman, both at home and abroad, what deservedly may be called "a yeoman's service." Until the middle of the eighteenth century only the rich in Britain enjoyed their jams and kindred sweets, for the reason that sugar was an imported luxury. It was the coming of cheap sugar from the West Indies, and the rise of the big jam houses, that made jam a common item of British fare, as well as one of Britain's proudest exports.

Fruit Pies

These recipes are for the English deep-dish pie. Although many recipes for fruit pies include a pastry lining as well as the top crust, our fruit pies were never pastry-lined.

A pastry funnel, or inverted egg-cup, was used to keep the crust raised only for soft fruit pies, such as raspberries, red and black currants, and blackberries. Other fruits, such as apples, plums, damsons and cherries needed no funnel, because the pastry cooked before the fruit was fully cooked, and there was no risk of the crust becoming sodden with fruit juice.

Pies were first put in the top of the oven to raise the crust; then in the bottom of the oven to allow the fruit to become fully cooked without spoiling the crust.

The regular pie crust was made with:

12 oz. flour
8 oz. butter (or half lard, and half butter)
a pinch of salt and a little water

Apple Pie

Peel the apples. Cut in halves and quarter. Remove the core. And cut each quarter in half.

The flavor of sliced apple is not as good as when only quartered and halved, since the juice boils out of the fruit before it is cooked, and the apples become tough and tasteless.

The apples should be sliced straight into the pie-dish (not first cut into a bowl of water), and piled high in the center, with sugar sprinkled throughout the layers.

Put on the crust, making a slit hole in the center for the steam to escape.

Bake approximately 1 hour. Serve with fine sugar and thick cream.

Other favorite fruit pies are black currant, blackberry with a small quantity of apple, and gooseberry.

Of these, black currant pie is considered one of the most typical English fruit pies, though I think that black currant pudding is far superior. Gooseberry pie is the traditional dessert for England's Whitsuntide—Whit Sunday lunch. At that season the gooseberries are young and green and hard. In this state they are also used for puddings, fools and for "bottling."

Fruit Puddings

Suet pastry is used for boiled fruit puddings.

1 lb. flour
6 oz. suet
a pinch of salt
a little milk or water

(1 lb. flour to 4 oz. of suet will make a plainer pudding, or what my mother would say "just a pudding.")

To make this pastry, rub very finely chopped suet into fine flour; mix with a little milk or water and the salt, and knead all well together by hand.

Line a pudding basin with the pastry and fill the center with whatever fruit is being used, allowing a generous sprinkling of sugar between each layer of fruit.

Cover either with waxed paper or a saucepan lid, and boil for 2½-3 hours.

Such puddings are made with:

Apples
Damsons
Blackberries, with a little apple added
Gooseberries

When cooked, the pudding basin is inverted on to the serving dish, leaving, if possible, an unbroken dome of pastry over the fruit. Serve with thick cream and soft sugar. Apple pudding is enhanced with a knob of butter ready for each serving.

It has been truly said that a well-risen boiled pudding takes a lot of beating. Gooseberry pudding, made properly from young fruit, has been extravagantly praised by gourmets. But damson pudding, to my mind, steals the show. It is rich and luxuriously colored beside the pale gooseberry. As the thick cream winds its

way into the out-flowing river of wine-dark juice upon your plate
there is nothing to remember except, like young green gooseberries, damsons demand a liberal sifting of fine sugar.

Apple Turnover which we called habitually and mistakenly, Apple Cake.

> Prepare the apples as for a pie. Roll out the pastry fairly thin,
> put the quartered apples on one half, sprinkle sugar on
> them, and turn the other half of pastry over the apples,
> envelope-wise, crinkling the two edges together. Make a
> hole on top as on any pie.

Apple Charlotte

This combination of bread and butter and apples is made with
small variations, according to a family's individual taste.

The standard recipe calls for a dish lined with thin slices of
stale white bread dipped in hot melted butter; the layers of apples
being interlined with more slices of the butter bread. In our
family breadcrumbs were always used instead of slices of bread.

> Butter a pie-dish.
> Cover the bottom thickly with crumbs of stale bread mixed
> with melted butter, then add a layer of apples sprinkled
> with sugar and grated lemon peel and lemon juice.
> Fill to the brim with alternate layers of breadcrumbs and
> apples, the bulk being apple, and the top covered thickly
> with breadcrumbs and dotted with butter.
> Bake covered until the apples have softened. Then remove
> the cover to allow the crumbs to crisp and brown.
> It is impossible to time exactly, depending on the cooking
> quality of the apples. But baking is approximately 1 hour.

Baked Apple and Apple Dumplings

These simple favorites need no recipe. But early in the year
the apples were baked whole with the cores left in, as they were
still tender and the pips gave a pleasant additional flavor. The
best apples should burst into a juicy fluff in about 15-20 minutes,
depending on their size.

Later in the year, the apples were cored, and a piece of bread stuffed into the hole at the bottom, and a mixture of butter, sugar and treacle poured in.

Apple Snow

Wash and dry 3 large cooking apples. Prick them in a few places and bake them in a moderately hot oven until they are soft.

Remove the skin and rub the pulp through a sieve. Beat the white of one egg to a froth, adding 3 oz. soft sugar, little by little. Then add the apple pulp and beat all together until thoroughly well mixed, light and soft.

Boston Apple Pie a speciality of Boston, Lincolnshire.

Cook until soft Codlin apples for choice, seasoning with a little cinnamon, a clove, and the rind of one lemon. Sieve the fruit, and mix sugar and butter—more or less according to taste—into the puree. Then add the yolks of 2 eggs and the white of 1; also the juice of a small lemon. Beat all thoroughly together and put into a pie dish lined with puff pastry. Decorate the edges. Bake ½ hour.

Gooseberry Amber is very similar to what was far more attractively named Gooseberry Tansy around 1700.

Cook gently 2 oz. of butter
1 lb. of prepared gooseberries
¼ lb. of soft sugar

When the fruit has become a soft, thick mass, stir in

1 oz. of fine breadcrumbs
The beaten yolks of 3 eggs

and turn the whole into a buttered pie dish.

Bake the mixture in a moderate oven for ½ hour.
Beat up the whites of the eggs to a very stiff froth.

Add 3 level tablespoonfuls of soft sugar.

Heap this mixture over the top, sprinkle in a little more soft sugar.

Bake in a cool oven until the mixture is a pale crisp brown.

If the fruit is very dry, it may be necessary to add another piece of butter.

If the fruit is gathered later in the season when it has become soft, it may be necessary to add more breadcrumbs.

The "tansy" should have the consistency of a solid omelette.

Other fruits, such as mulberries and loganberries, also make good "tansies."

Gooseberry Queen Pudding

Put 1 lb. of prepared gooseberries in a pie dish with very little water, and sugar to taste, adding a little grated lemon peel.

When cooked pour over the following mixture, and bake in a moderate oven until a nice brown:

1 well-beaten egg

1 dessertspoonful flour

1 teacup of fine breadcrumbs

Sugar to taste, and a small teacup of milk.

Add, at the last moment, a good pinch of baking powder.

The mixture should be prepared a little time before using, so that the breadcrumbs may be properly soaked. Like the Tansy, other stewed fruit may be substituted for gooseberries.

Gooseberry Fool

This is an old English sweet. In spite of an epicure's praise for gooseberry pudding, as children gooseberry fool was our favorite gooseberry dessert—we must have eaten gallons of it, and it is well worth the tedium of preparing the little green fruit, topping and tailing them.

Whipped cream was an essential ingredient once upon a time. Nowadays, custard is a generally accepted compromise.

Cook 1 quart of green gooseberries in a close-covered pan
until tender and a soft pulp.

Rub the pulp through a sieve, and add enough sugar to
sweeten sufficiently while the pulp is still hot.

Allow to become quite cold. Fold in a pint of cold whipped
cream or custard. This quantity of cream or custard varies
slightly, since it is important that the fruit pulp and the
cream or custard be the same consistency, so that they all
combine to become a soft billowy mass.

Gooseberry fool is always served cold.

Damson Fool

Boil together for 5 minutes 3 dessertspoonfuls of brown sugar
and ½ gill of water.

Add 1½ pints of damsons and cook the whole until the fruit
is reduced to a pulp.

Rub the fruit pulp through a sieve to remove the stones and
skins, and then mix with a pint of custard.

Leave the mixture in a cool place to thicken; pour it into
small custard glasses, and serve with a topping of whipped
cream.

Summer Pudding

This might well be called Simple Pudding, but because it is so
simple to make, it is worth making carefully and well.

Bread is used instead of pastry to line the bowl, and the fruits
used are loganberries, or red and white currants with raspberries,
or blackberries.

Butter a deep pudding basin and line it with bread.

The bread should be cut in a round to fit the bottom of the
basin, and the bread slices cut on a slope to dovetail them
together in fitting the sides of the basin. These should all
be pressed firmly into place.

The fruit should be boiled in sufficient sugar, and when boiling "lifted" directly into the basin, packing it in carefully.

Then fill up the basin with the berry juice, and add any odd
scraps of sliced bread left over. Fit either a plate or saucer
on the top of the basin to press down the fruit. Put a weight

on it, and leave until the following day, when the pudding is turned out on to a dish and served with sugar and cream.

Apple Cheese

Apple cheese is, in effect, the stiffest form of apple butter.

Peel and core sufficient apples to allow 2 lbs. of apples after the peel and cores have been removed.

Stew the fruit until quite soft.

Rub through a sieve (we used the old hair sieves) with a wooden spoon.

Add 1¼ lbs. of sugar
1 teaspoonful of golden coloring (cochineal)
a little bruised ginger tied up in a small muslin bag
the thin rind and juice of half a lemon.

Boil all together for about an hour. Take out the ginger, and pour into shaped moulds. When cold cover with paraffin wax, or in the old-fashioned way with a piece of paper cut into a round and sealed down with flour paste.

(The thin rind and juice of 2 lemons is enough for 10 lbs. of apple pulp).

Apple cheese improves with keeping up to a year, and will keep up to two years. Regarded as a winter sweet, it is served with blanched almonds stuck in its amber gold, and garnished with whipped cream or custard.

Damson Cheese

Set 5 or 6 lbs. of damsons to 1 quart of water in a stone jar. Let them cook slowly, until the fruit is tender and the juice runs.

Rub the fruit through a sieve, and add:
1 lb. of sugar to every 1 lb. of fruit pulp.

(The sugar should be warmed in the oven while the fruit is being sieved).

Boil well until the mixture jellies, then put the cheese into straightsided jars, and tie down in the usual way, or with brandied paper over the top before sealing.

The best damson cheese is made by saving the stones extracted when the fruit is sieved, cracking them and adding the kernels to the pulp. This gives a strong almond flavor to the juice. (A shortcut to this perfection is to add only a few kernels to the pulp, or a few sweet almonds).

The cheese, if properly made, is almost black, cutting a deep purple, and should keep for years.

Damson Pickle—a sweet pickle

4 quarts damsons
1 quart white vinegar
2 lbs. loaf sugar
¼ lb. peppercorns
¼ lb. cloves

> Put the vinegar, sugar and spices into a preserving pan.
> When the mixture boils, add the damsons.
> Boil until they begin to crush and split—usually in about 5-7 minutes.
> Bottle, and when cold, seal down.

Lemon Cheese or Curd

This old English favorite seems little known in America today. Although *The Williamsburg Art of Cookery* gives three recipes for lemon cheese, Fanny Farmer's nearest approach to it is as a lemon filling for tarts. Her ingredients are 4 egg yolks, 4 tablespoons sugar and 4 tablespoons lemon juice.

The Hyde lemon cheese was stored from February until December, in the *cool*, dry jam cupboard, and the jars were set to lie on their sides. In steam-heated houses lemon cheese would not keep so long, on account of its butter content, and should probably be kept under refrigeration.

1 lb. loaf sugar
6 egg yolks and 2 egg whites
Juice of 3 lemons; grated rind of 2
¼ lb. butter

> Wipe the lemons, and rub the loaf sugar on the rinds so that the sugar may absorb the rind oil.

Melt the butter in the top of a double saucepan.
Add the lemon juice and the grated rind, and the sugar.
When these are dissolved, add the well-beaten eggs.
Allow the mixture to simmer, not boil, stirring all the time.
When it is as thick as honey, pour into jars.
When quite cold, seal well.

Note

The following compromises will still result in a rich curd:
Granulated sugar may be used instead of loaf sugar; being
   easier and quicker to dissolve.
4 eggs may be used instead of six—4 yolks and the white of 1.

Our cook

The Boar's head

12. Sweet and Savoury

In writing of the english character, Sir Arthur Bryant quotes a somewhat bemused Frenchman on the pudding:

> "The pudding is a dish very difficult to be described, because of the several sorts there are of it . . . They bake them in an oven, they boil them with meat, they make them fifty several ways . . . Ah what an excellent thing is an *English pudding!*" *

There are people who say that puddings and pies are the unshakable foundation of the English cuisine, that when in doubt the English cook turns to the pudding with the determination of the magnetic needle to point North. Christmas Pudding, Yorkshire Pudding—capitalized with a respect comparable to that shown the Queen—and suet puddings are the best known among what the Frenchman called the several sorts.

Nobody can say how long Britons have been eating Christmas pudding, but it certainly dates back to when the boar's head was the main meat dish of the feast and the Christmas turkey was still among the mists of centuries to come. It is, of course, the plum pudding, and was made well in advance of Yuletide, in my old home usually in November. Then everyone in the house took a share in stirring the rich ingredients, thus earning the right to taste them with a critical tongue and to make a wish as they did

* Arthur Bryant, *The National Character*, 1934.

so. By custom, the cook slipped into the mix—secretly—an assortment of small silver coins and charms in enough number to assure every eater of the pudding at least one. To get a thimble in one's slice of Christmas pudding was to draw the symbol of an old maid; a button betokened the bachelor, a little silver pig meant good luck, and a silver coin was a promise of a bag of silver and gold. Christmas was not Christmas without its Christmas pudding.

Our recipe for the pudding was among those things "passed down" from one generation to another, each adding its bit of culinary lore. Somewhere along the line in our family a cook had seen fit to depart from the strictly traditional by mixing into the pudding a small portion of grated raw carrots; the addition made our puddings a trifle lighter and offset a little of their richness. Also, apparently, at sometime in the past a cook had decided that our Christmas plum pudding would be a better pudding without plums, so that you will find no plums in my mother's old recipe, which I give later. For that matter, after search, I can find plums prescribed in only one recipe set forth for the ancient plum pudding by English authorities on the subject. That is in the recipe of the Royal Family of George I, which calls for "plums 1 lb. stoned and cut in half."

But today the detail of no plums in plum pudding is hardly of more than academic concern even to devotees of the old-time Christmas feast, when the steaming hot pudding was marched in with ceremony, a sprig of holly flying like the flag of Empire from its summit. Duly anointed with fine brandy, the match applied, the pudding would flame in glory—a glory that now comes to us in tin cans.

When I consider the long hours of work that went into those old-home puddings, and the seven hours of boiling, I use the term "tin can" with due respect. If the modern tin can needs vindication, some at least may be found in today's canned Christmas puddings, plums or no plums. Served hot with a really good sauce, it is a task for an expert to detect any difference between the good canned pudding and the best home creation. All that is missing are the silver coins and charms.

Just as it wasn't Christmas without its plumless plum pudding, it was hardly Christmas without mincemeat pie, and our mince pie *did* contain meat, as well as currants and other fruits, and a liberal dose of brandy. The mince pie is probably as old as Norman England. Samuel Pepys records that for Christmas Day, 1666, he arose in the morning "leaving my wife desirous to sleep, having sat up till four this morning seeing her mayds make mincepies." Mrs. Pepys was in the tradition of many generations of English housewives.

The English mince pie is a small individual affair, not a capacious family-size as in America; a small round of pastry is cut for the bottom half, a similar round for the top, and the pie is baked in tartlet tins—in big families by the dozens of pies. To eat twelve mince pies between Christmas day and Twelfth Night is supposed to be reliable insurance for twelve lucky months ahead.

The English Trifle, which in fact is no trifle, is another festive dish in the sense that it is an elegant and rich party-sweet. The name is a grand understatement. For the true Trifle—a glorified Tipsy cake—there is no simplified substitute. It should be made in a crystal dish, and include sponge galettes flavored with sherry or madeira wine; also custard and jam, whipped cream, blanched almonds, glace cherries, and ratafias or silver dollar-size macaroons.

To go from the Trifle to Roly-Poly pudding is to drop from the sublime, as good English cooks do with ease, to hard earth, like Cinderella returning to her kitchen after the Fairy Ball. Roly-Polys are good solid hunger-stoppers for a winter's day, and belong to old-time yeoman's fare. Of suet crust rolled into long, smooth strips, they are spread with treacle or jam; when spread with raisins they went by the name of Dog-in-the-Blanket—rolled up with the edges pinched together to keep the filling in, and boiled steadily in a pudding cloth for at least an hour.

Rice pudding can be so, so good, and it can be so, so ordinary.

It was not until after cheap rice was brought in to England from Carolina duty-free in 1796 that it became popular. Since then, rice has provided a standby nursery-pudding for generations of English children.

Out of curiosity I have often, in browsing through books in a book store, looked up the directions for making this most simple of all puddings. Almost without exception, the most important instruction is confined to a haphazard note: cook until done. The secret of making a good rice pudding, providing the milk is really creamy, is to cook it in a very slow oven for a very long time, long after it is "done." In old houses rice pudding was left cooking slowly on the hob for hours. The recipe I give produced a pudding that we loved; deliciously creamy, the top all gold and brown, baked four hours in a slow oven.

By no means are pancakes an English invention, but by custom they have been tossed for long centuries on the English Shrove Tuesday, and are accorded far more dignity than in many other countries. In England pancakes are never served flat, piled in stacks; instead each cake is rolled up and served by itself, sprinkled with sugar and with its own small slice of lemon beside it. The individually treated pancake has been called a symbol of the Englishman's insularity. He goes further and regards each pancake as a pudding.

The Queen of Puddings, which is a name and not an effusion, is definitely English, though unless most carefully prepared and good materials only are used, it becomes a soggy and feeble plebeian. It is made by general preference with breadcrumbs, eggs to form a vanilla-flavored custard, and raspberry jam. Properly compounded, and served with a delicately browned meringue topping, it can be royal indeed.

Personally I rate Bakewell pudding as more deserving of the title of Queen. It is named Bakewell not because it needs to be especially well-baked—though it should be baked well—but because it originated at Bakewell in the Peak District of Derbyshire. The story goes that the hostess of the Rutland Arms, a coaching

inn at Bakewell, gave instructions to her cook to prepare a rich
jam tart for her guests, stipulating that the pastry should be mixed
with a liquid consisting of beaten egg and melted butter.

After dinner, the guests sent for the hostess to compliment her
on the meal, especially the pudding. But why pudding, she asked
herself, when she had given the cook such precise instructions
for a jam tart? The cook was questioned, and confessed that she
had got muddled. She had made an ordinary puff paste, and
spread it with jam; then, remembering the mixture of beaten eggs
and melted butter, but not knowing what to do with it, had simply
poured it on top.

The cook promised never to do such a thing again. "On the
contrary," the hostess said firmly, "you will continue to do what
you did time and time again."

At our home Bakewell pudding was, I think, just about our top
favorite, and my mother made it superbly well, even by the critical
standards set by her sisters. I have compared her recipe with
many others: she used an extravagant five eggs instead of the
usual two to three eggs, and included ground almonds and jam,
whereas some recipes call for preserved fruit and omit the almonds.

So much for puddings, or should I say, so little? Among the
bemused Frenchman's "fifty several" I have touched on only a
few, putting discretion before valor. England's infinitude of puddings must be met on their home soil to be enjoyed, and discovery
is one facet of that enjoyment. They may, like the Yorkshire pudding, be no pudding at all—note that I have discussed that famous
"pudding" under meats, though how it is made is among the
recipes that close this chapter; again, the pudding that you discover will, the chances are, be a much different dish than en-
counters with it elsewhere than in England have led you to expect.

The Yorkshire pudding recipe that I have chosen furnishes a
good example of what too often happens to English puddings that
are copied abroad. My chosen recipe, which produces the real
thing, is simplicity itself. Now, just for the fun of it, check the

recipe with any non-English cook book. Check, too, the recipes for English Trifle. Unless the book that you check is well above average, you will discover discrepancies in both ingredients and methods of making. For instance, the beaten eggs should be poured into the flour, in making Yorkshire pudding—the flour should not be mixed into the eggs.

Generally, simplicity marks all English cooking, and puddings or no, the English tooth is not sweet, at least not nearly so sweet as the American. That fact explains the Yorkshire's affinity with meat, the down-to-earth quality of the Roly-Polys, and what otherwise would appear to be a most mystifying twist of the British taste. Your typical English gourmet prefers the piquant and the pungent, mint sauce to mint jelly, sharp mustard undisguised to the blandly mixed, and he likes his ham straight, undespoiled by sugar and spice and rings of pineapple.

Such preferences explain that purely English addition to a dinner, the Savoury. To many an Englishman this is the fondly cherished crowning morsel of a meal. Though savouries may be served as appetizers at the beginning of dinner, they are customarily served between the main course and dessert, or make the end of a meal and so take the place of the dessert.

Most savouries can be used, too, as hot or cold *hors d'oeuvre*. Their chief ingredients are derived largely from among fish and shell fish: shrimps, prawns, lobsters, and crabs; oysters and smoked salmon; anchovies and sardines, hard roes of herring and cod. Other ingredients may be mushrooms, chicken livers, ham or bacon and kidneys; eggs and cheese. One unchanging feature is the essentially English foundation of crisp toast, spread with ordinary or savoury butters.

As a rule each savoury goes by the name of its chief ingredient, so that you know instantly what you are going to eat. Three of the best, however, have completely misguiding titles. Welsh Rarebit, commonly called "rabbit" is the supreme way to eat toasted cheese but has nothing of the rabbit or of Wales about it. Nor has Scotch Woodcock, a universal favorite, any relationship with either Scotland or the gamebird of that name; it consists of scrambled egg, anchovy fillets and anchovy paste. Angels on Horseback, in the opinion of many, is the finest savoury of all; it consists of oysters wrapped in rashers of bacon and grilled, not of horsemeat as I once heard a young lady venture to guess on shipboard.

Of all shell fish and salt-water fish, the anchovy is the most versatile. It is a small, herring-like fish caught in large quantities in the Mediterranean and the English Channel. Fillets of anchovies, served as garnishings and appetizers, are universally known. But the anchovy essences and pastes have long been English specialities.

Indeed the anchovy might be called the backbone of the savoury—and an excellent appetizer for the cocktail hour. Homemade anchovy butter and its commercial counterpart, anchovy paste, have been used as spreads for teatime toast and sandwiches and for dinner savouries for a long time. Anchovy essence, which is the essential flavoring of Anchovy Sauce makes a very English fine fish sauce. I have already mentioned the subtle use of this essence in the famous Melton Mowbray Pork Pie.

An incomparable relish, the anchovy in any form must be used discreetly. One of today's anchovy specialists in turning it out wholesale in a factory even gives the somewhat strange sales advice to use the essence and paste most sparingly, because their flavor is then "more defined."

Fortunes have been made from the diminutive anchovy. Several British food-product firms market their own brands of pastes and essences, and at least two London houses qualify as anchovy specialists: John Burgess & Son Ltd., who claim to have originated anchovy essence, and C. Osborn & Sons, the anchovy paste and Patum Peperium, popularly known as The Gentleman's Relish.

The House of Burgess, founded in 1760, has a proud record. That year, William Burgess, a country grocer, sent his son John to London, to set up in trade as an "Oilman and Italian Ware-houseman," or in today's language as a delicatessen shopkeeper. John prospered. Among other items of delicatessen, he invented his "Original and Superior Essence of Anchovy." He inserted his advertisement in the first issue of *The Times,* on January 1, 1778, and of all the commercial undertakings represented in that first issue of what is now *The London Times,* the House of Burgess alone survives.

Lord Byron and Sir Walter Scott both extolled the fish sauces obtainable at "Burgess' in the Strand"; Lord Nelson took Burgess' delicacies with him to the Battle of the Nile; a daughter of King George III allowed her royal warrant to be displayed on the "Original Fish Sauce Warehouse," which was eventually pulled down when the ever-growing Burgess' business was moved to its present home in Hythe Road.

John Burgess died in 1820. Amidst such world-shaking events as Wolfe's capture of Quebec, loss of the American Colonies, the French Revolution and the Napoleonic Wars, he had continued to import salad oil, truffles, olives, and the best Italian anchovies from Gorgona, off Leghorn. His heirs expanded the business until now Burgess both imports and exports, the little brown seal label, "A John Burgess Product," going forth to most of the world.

C. Osborn & Sons was founded by the London grocer, John Osborn, in 1828. In his spare time he loved to try out various concoctions on his customers, and his anchovy paste soon found favor. It sold so well in London that he placed it on the Paris market as Pâte D'Anchois à la Francaise, to the delight of French epicures. His second appetizer, The Gentleman's Relish, made from anchovies—which he and his heirs have always obtained from the North coast of Spain—butter, cereal and spices, assured undying fame to his house.

Osborn's trade today solely as anchovy specialists under the initial C instead of J, for Charles Osborn who succeeded his father in the business. The shallow white glazed pots in which they pack their Anchovy Paste and A Gentleman's Relish for the home market are identical with the pots used in 1828. For reasons of weight, fragility and better preservation of the contents, other pots are used for their overseas trade.

"Preservation" is a fetish of Osborn's. They assure their customers that the contents of their small jars, once opened, will keep for three weeks, and of the large jars for two months, providing they are kept in a cool, dry place, but *not* in a refrigerator.

Unopened pots will keep ten years or longer. This added virtue of anchovies makes them ideal camping appetizers, and explains why both Burgess' and Osborn's anchovy products have been included in such historic events as the Battle of the Nile, explorations of the Antartic and Everest Expeditions to the top of the world. Though the sun may today, here or there, actually set on the British flag, the ubiquitous savoury has made no such concession as yet to dwindling empire.

Christmas Pudding

Ranging through various recipes for Christmas Puddings, from King George I's and Mrs. Beeton's pudding, the ingredients are almost invariably the same, and the differences in various recipes occur only in the differing proportions. Our own home recipe, likewise, followed the same ingredient pattern with one difference. A small quantity of grated carrots was included, and was considered to make the puddings lighter.

7 oz. flour
14 oz. finely shredded beef suet
14 oz. currants
½ lb. seedless raisins
10 oz. sultanas
½ lb. brown sugar
½ lemon
3 eggs
1 oz. ground almonds

½ teaspoonful mixed spice
½ teaspoonful nutmeg
½ lb. mixed candied peel
    (orange and lemon)
7 oz. breadcrumbs
¼ lb. carrots
¼ pint of old ale
a wineglassful of brandy

Mix the flour and the salt and spices. Then the breadcrumbs
and the grated raw carrots, and the rest of the ingredients
except the brandy and ale, the lemon juice and eggs.

Leave to stand overnight.

Next day add the eggs, well-beaten, first, the lemon juice,
the ale and brandy. Mix well so that the mixture is stiff
but not too moist.

Place in buttered basins. Cover with a piece of buttered
paper and tie down with cloths.

Boil 7 hours.

Mince Pies

"The Hyde" recipe for mincemeat was certainly intended to
provide for the proverbial 12 pies per person between Christmas
and Twelfth Night. Although the old recipes all include "minced"
meat this appears to have been dropped from today's recipes.

6 lbs. currants, washed and dried

2 lbs. lean beef, well boiled and minced

4 lbs. sugar

3 lbs. very finely chopped suet

6 lbs. of raisins stoned and minced.

6 large apples

1 lb. lemon peel (candied)

1½ pints of brandy

The brandy is added last to the well mixed ingredients. The
mincemeat is then put into earthen jars, and tied closely.

Queen of Puddings

1 large cupful of breadcrumbs

½ small cupful of sugar

2 eggs

1 pint of milk

the grated rind of 1 lemon

Separate the whites from the egg yolks. Beat the yolks well
and mix with a pint of milk.

Pour on to the breadcrumbs and sugar, and grated lemon
rind, and mix all well together.

Bake in a moderate oven.

When cool cover with jam. Pile over the beaten egg whites,
and bake in oven until a golden color.

Bakewell Pudding

¼ *lb. puff paste*   6 *oz. sugar*
5 *eggs*   ¼ *lb. butter*
1 *oz. almonds*   *jam*

Cover or line a dish with thin pastry.

Put over this a layer of jam ½″ thick (apricot is very good for
this).

Put the yolks of 5 eggs and the white of one egg into a basin
and beat well.

Add the sugar and butter (which should be melted first); and
grated almonds. Beat all together until thoroughly mixed.

Pour the mixture into the dish over the jam, and bake in a
moderate oven until soft and creamy and a delicate brown:
15 minutes first in a hot oven, and 25 minutes in a reduced
heat.

English Trifle

Trifle should be made in a crystal bowl—at least a deep glass
dish.

8 *sponge cakes—lady-fingers*
4 *spoonfuls Raspberry jam*
2 *eggs*   ⎱—*sugar for sweetening and sherry for flavoring the*
½ *pint milk* ⎰   *custard*
½ *pint whipped cream & sherry also to flavor the cream*
ratafias or macaroons
split, blanched almonds
pink & white sugar decorets—known in England as Hundreds
  & Thousands

Cut the sponge cakes in half and place in the glass dish.

Pour in sufficient sherry to soak them nicely.

Make a sweetened custard, and flavor it with sherry (or brandy) and pour it hot over the sponge fingers.

When quite cold, stud the custard thickly with split blanched almonds.

Add the top layering of thickly whipped cream.

Decorate with ratafias round the edge, glace cherries and more almonds over the top, and add a final sprinkle of sugar decorets.

Yorkshire Pudding

4 *tablespoonfuls of flour*   *2 eggs*
½ *pint of milk, and a shade over*   *a little salt*
1 *tablespoonful of water*

Put the flour in a basin, making a well in the center.

Gradually mix in half of the milk.

Break in the eggs. Beat well. Add the rest of the milk.

The mixture should then "rest" an hour.

Whisk a tablespoonful of water into the batter.

Pour the mixture into a shallow tin which has already been made hot in the oven, and greased with some of the dripping from the meat.

Bake in a hot oven for 15 minutes, and then brown on the top shelf for another 5 minutes, when it is puffy, crisp and brown, and ready to be served instantly with the meat.

Yorkshire Pudding is not only an accompaniment of roast beef. It is good with any meat roast.

In Yorkshire the pudding is usually served before the meat.

In Lancashire it is usually served after the meat course—with a little castor sugar.

Suet Puddings—Roly-Polys

1¼ *lb. flour*
½ *lb. of finely chopped beef suet*
½ *teaspoonful salt*
Cold water to mix or, for a richer pudding, egg and milk

Mix all together, and roll out the dough.

Spread with jam.

Wet the edges and roll up the pudding, pinching the edges together.

Roll up in a floured cloth, tie the ends tightly together, and boil for 2 to 2½ hours.

Sometimes this pudding was spread with raisins, and was called Dog-in-the-Blanket.

Rice Pudding

2 oz. rice

1 pint milk

2 oz. sugar

1 oz. butter

Sprinkle the rice in the bottom of the pie-dish.

Sprinkle the sugar over the rice; add the butter.

Pour in the milk and stir well.

Set to bake in a very slow oven.

The secret of a creamy rice pudding is in the slow and long baking. Mrs. Beeton sets 2 hours for this, but 4 hours is better.

Pancakes

2 oz. flour

1 egg

¼ pint of milk

2 oz. clarified fat for frying

2 oz. soft sugar

lemon juice and a pinch of salt

Mix the flour and salt together, and make into a batter with the egg and milk.

Heat the frying-pan, add a little fat.

When quite hot, pour in enough batter to cover the pan thinly.

When golden brown on one side, toss or turn and fry the other.

Squeeze a little lemon juice over it; dust with soft sugar, roll up and serve with another dusting of soft sugar.

Welsh Rarebit

Put two large tablespoonfuls of ale into a saucepan.

Add a small lump of butter, 4 oz. of grated cheese (Cheddar or Cheshire), season with pepper, salt and made English mustard to taste.

Melt the cheese in the ale slowly, stirring all to a thick, creamy paste.

When thoroughly hot, but not boiling, pour the mixture on to slices of well buttered, freshly made toast.

Brown lightly for a second under the grill.

Angels on Horseback

Make ready some very thin rashers of bacon.
Cut them in half across, and in each half wrap an oyster.
Skewer or tie them.
Grill, and serve very hot on small pieces of buttered toast.

Scotch Woodcock

This consists of buttered toast spread with anchovy paste, and piled with creamy scrambled egg, and finally topped with thin strips of anchovy fillets added at the last moment. Older recipes are more painstaking, and use chopped anchovies instead of anchovy paste.

The proportions used to 4 slices of bread are as follows:

7 *anchovies*
4 *eggs*
½ *pint of cream*

Wash, scrape and finely chop anchovies, and spread them between two slices of well toasted buttered bread.

Meanwhile the egg yolks, beaten with the cream and seasoned with cayenne pepper and salt should be ready.

Set the creamed yolks over the fire to thicken; carefully to
see they do not boil.

Pour over the toast and serve as hot as possible.

Shrimp Paste or Potted Shrimps

Melt ¼ lb. of butter in a saucepan.

Season with a little mace, cayenne pepper, and a speck of
anchovy sauce.

Heat 1 pint of shelled shrimps gently and thoroughly in the
seasoned butter, but do not let them boil, as this toughens
the shrimps. When the shrimps are impregnated with the
butter, pour the mixture into small pots and seal with
clarified butter.

Anchovy Paste

4 oz. butter

4 egg yolks

6 tablespoonfuls of anchovy essence

¼ teaspoonful cayenne pepper

Cream the butter.

Beat in egg yolks.

Mix in the anchovy essence and pepper.

Heat, but do not allow to boil, and stir all the time until the
mixture thickens.

Put into pots.

When cold, seal with clarified butter.

Anchovy Cheese

This has been a favorite savoury for two hundred years or so.

Fry half-inch thick slices of bread and butter, and cut them
into fingers.

Set a boned anchovy fillet on each finger.

Grate some cheese, and mix it with a little chopped parsley,
and spread it on the fingers fairly thickly.

Pour over a little melted butter, arrange the fingers in a fire-
proof dish, and brown them under the grill.

Anchovy Toasts

Slices of bread fried in clarified butter may be spread either with Anchovy Paste, and served with filleted anchovies, or Montpelier Butter.

True anchovy toasts are a little more trouble.

Fillets of anchovy in oil, pounded up with butter—the same amount of each.

The mixture is spread on squares of toast or fried bread, and two anchovy fillets set cross-wise on each square.

Sprinkle with chopped yolk of egg mixed with a little chopped parsley and chives.

Anchovy Eggs

Anchovy essence or pounded anchovies make excellent stuffed eggs.

Savoury Butters

Montpelier Butter

Blanch for 2 minutes in boiling water 2 handfuls of fresh mixed herbs:

Parsley
Watercress
Tarragon
Chervil
A few spinach leaves
A small amount of chives (or chopped shallots).

Drain, cool, chop finely and pound in a mortar. Mix into this:

6 oz. butter
2 anchovy fillets
a little pickled gherkin
a teaspoonful of capers, chopped finely

Stir and add seasoning:

salt
cayenne pepper
lemon juice
and, if wished, a hint of olive oil

A stiff creamy mixture results.

Green Butter

Wash and bone 2 oz. of anchovies.

Boil a handful of green parsley for five minutes in a very little water.

Strip the parsley from the stalks: chop it very fine.

Beat parsley, anchovies and ¼ lb. butter together into a paste.

Pot and seal.

Dr. Oliver's biscuits

13. Britons' Oldest Friend

"No BREAD?" cried *Punch* of London a century ago. "Then bring me some toast!"

Bread is to your true Englishman what spaghetti is to the Italian or curds are to the Greek. It is the Briton's oldest and dearest friend whenever and wherever the bugle calls to mess. He may quaff down his pint of cider or ale, relish his bite of favorite cheese, lay to with a will on a well-roasted joint, relish his savoury, but the old-faithful closest to his elbow at mealtime is the crowning triumph of the wheat.

181

"I like to eat my meat in good company, Sir."

"So do I, and the best company for meat is bread. A sandwich is better company than a fool." *

Not any bread; English bread! It is as different from American, French or Italian bread as London is from New York, Paris or Rome. Close-textured, plain, firm—London-like might well describe it—bread is the most humble and yet the most prized item of the Briton's board. "Bread to strengthen man's heart" is evoked in The Book of Common Prayer.

Even in the eighteenth century, well-fed French travelers, themselves great patrons of their own national bread, remarked on the quality and texture of English bread: on the buttered slices that were cut "as thin as poppy leaves," and on the bread that was crisped and browned by the fire and buttered hot for tea. "This is called toast," one admiring traveler noted, and found it "incomparably good." **

Plain or toasted, there was—and is—bread on the table or the sideboard of every English meal. We had it at breakfast as toast, golden toast set in the time-honored "toast-rack" to remain crisp until we were ready to spread it with butter and marmalade. At lunch or dinner, whether anyone wanted it or not, the cottage loaf sat sedately on its traditional round wooden bread-board, which was carved along its edge with ears of wheat, and a sharp, broad silver-handled knife was always ready beside the board. Unfailingly there was bread and butter for tea, and we children were supposed to eat at least one slice of bread before launching into cake.

To me, it never seemed at all unreal that Bread was one of the live characters in Maeterlinck's The Blue Bird. "I shall always be there," he promised Tyltyl and Mytyl in farewell as they were about to leave the dream world at dawn, "in the breadpan, on the shelf, on the table, beside the soup, I who am, if I may say so,

---

* Mrs. C. F. Leyel and Miss Olga Hartley, The Gentle Art of Cookery, 1925.
** C. P. Moritz, A Journey to England, 1782.

with Water and Fire, the most faithful companion, the oldest
friend of Man."

My daily bread, as a youngster, was baker's bread which the
baker delivered every other day, carrying it in a big wicker basket
on his arm. There was the long-cut tin loaf and the shorter but
higher plain tin loaf; the twist or collar, the four-pointed-corner
Coburg, and the comfortable looking cottage loaf, which was invariably our choice. But good as baker's bread might be, home-
made bread, as my mother made it, was and still is best.

On special occasions she went through the slow but simple
process, filled the kitchen with the warm yeasty fragrance of
baking bread, and turned out in triumph four two-pound cottage
loaves. This was the kind of bread that Tennyson described as a
"dusky loaf that smelt of home." I give her recipe, a standard
one to this day, at the end of the chapter.

My mother maintained that the trick of baking bread, honest
English home-baked bread, was not in the simple ingredients but
the way they are handled, modelled as closely as possible on the
old ritual. She declared that no bread she made was ever quite as
good as the bread baked at her old home, The Hyde, of home-
grown wheat, and baked in the old-fashioned brick oven.

She would recall the bags of wheat being taken to the nearby
water mill, and the resulting flour brought back in gleaming white
bags and emptied, as needed, into the great flour bin in the
kitchen; the medium white flour going in to the larger division in
the bin, the very white flour in the smaller half.

Saturday was the weekly baking day, and preparations were
made the night before. Sufficient medium white flour to make
twelve two-and-a-half pound loaves was put into the one round
wooden tub, and enough of the very white flour to make ten two-
and-a-half pound loaves was put into another tub. A hole was
then made in the middle of each pile of flour, and yeast that had
been mixed with milk-warm water poured into it. A spoon was
then worked around the outside rim of the yeasty oasis until it
came to the consistency of a thin batter. Flour was then sprinkled

over the batter holes and the wooden lids put on, and the yeast left to do its work overnight in the warm kitchen.

By morning the batter had cracked the thin covering of flour, and the whole mass was ready to form into dough. Fisted, rolled over, pressed out, folded up and pressed again the dough was worked into a big round. A little dry flour was once more thinly scattered, the lids put on so that the dough was kept warm to ferment for another fifteen to twenty minutes before being made into loaves. These were the traditional cottage loaves, a comfortable looking shape, with its small dented bun atop the larger bottom crust. The round bottom portion and the twisted round of the top were all of a piece, and a final pressing of the thumb made a little dent in the crown.

By this time the oven had been made "ready," and a ready oven, which an experienced baker could test by putting her face within a yard of its front, was considered half the art of good baking. Of brick, it was fired with dry fagot sticks. When the strong, lively fire had heated the oven sufficiently for the bricks to retain their heat and then gradually and automatically cool off, the hot wood coals were swept out, and the oven cleaned by a cloth wrapped mop-like around a long thick stick. The loaves, packed ready on a steel plate attached to a long pole, were put in the far end of the oven. After an hour, pans of apple turn-overs and plain plum cakes were slipped in to the space left at the mouth of the oven. In another hour bread and cakes were done, and the loaves taken out and put upside down on the top of the bin to cool.

Old-timers among country bakers still insist, as my mother did, that no bread equalled that which was baked in the wood-heated brick oven. And there are many who declare that no flour equals the unprocessed flour from home-grown wheat. But, keeping in step with the pace of the tin can era, people have devised effective short-cut methods in making bread, and thought up ingenious ways of keeping the dough warm by tucking a bowl of it into the corner of the sofa banked with pillows, and setting a bowl of dough in a bigger bowl of hot water, covering it with a newspaper and placing it in front of the gas fire in the sitting room with an air of It Can Be Done!

Few "finished" foods bring to mind so many country scenes as does a cottage loaf: grain or cornfields a continuing sea of green through summer days until the oats yellow to pale straw, and the bearded barley and the wheat become burnished gold under the Midas touch of the August sun. In England, corn does not mean maize as it does in America, for Europe has no maize. England's corn came out of ancient Egypt, a trinity: oats, barley, and above all wheat. These are the Big Three, and corn harvest is the coronation of the farmer's year.

Like the old-fashioned brick bread oven, the old ways of harvesting are fast disappearing. Wonderful machines now throw out the winnowed grain in sacks where once the scattered sheaves were gathered by hand, and set up in stooks, eight sheaves to a stook, and set pillarwise across the harvest field. In due course the sheaves were built into a massive rick at the side of the field or in the rickyard, and crowned with a sharp-pitched roof of thatch until the humming thresher came to sift the grain from the chaff.

I see all this in the cottage loaf. If there is one sight above all others that abides more firmly in mind, it is the sight of a field at harvest time, completely colonnaded, stook by stook, with corn. There was sweat and toil as well as beauty in such old-time harvesting, in that hand-reaping of the manna from heaven which, since Moses led his people out of Egypt, has filled the dreams of hungry men.

Bread is something the average housewife holds in holy respect and is reluctant to waste, even to the crumbs. Breadcrumbs, well sifted and toasted, can be kept jar-tight and ready to use for layerings and toppings in a multitude of dishes. Also, seasoned with herbs, they make the basis for all stuffings and forcemeat. "Brown crumbs"—white breadcrumbs gently fried in butter to a golden brown and served on a dish as a heap of crisp, rich brown crumbs—we considered one of the essential accompaniments to roast pheasant, partridge and roast chicken; the perfect marriage with bread sauce. Croutons, the French word for square, diced or cubed stale bread, fried in butter, are wonderful additions to thick cream soups. And cubed bread, fried in hot salad oil, goes well in a garlic-rubbed bowl of lettuce, grated cheese, egg yolks and lemon juice; a salad that is a meal in itself.

Biscuit and cheese—or as Americans say, crackers and cheese— are but a step removed from bread and cheese. The word "biscuit" was coined from the French *bis-cuit* and means twice-cooked bread, or as the dictionary defines it, flat cakes of bread baked crisp and dry.

Originally the hardtack-type ship's biscuit was made to provide for the necessities of sailors and soldiers, and all travelers on long voyages. It was the fare for mediaeval monks in times of special devotion when they were not supposed to take time off for cooking and baking. And although the French invented the name, the English for a very long time now have been recognized as master bakers of a wide range of biscuits which bear little resemblance to the old hardtack, founder of the family.

Biscuit is a word that means different things on the two sides of the Atlantic. In England biscuits fall into two groups, sweet and plain. The sweet biscuits—"cookies" in America—are only rarely home-made today; along with the plain or cheese biscuit, so called because it is eaten with cheese at the end of a meal in lieu of, or in addition to dessert, they are now almost entirely factory made. This is a tribute to the commercial biscuit makers' art. In common with other famous brands of commercially produced British food, the factory-made biscuit has its long established lines that wend back to some original home-made recipe.

The Bath Oliver is but one example. There are other biscuits which are called Bath Olivers besides those made by Fortt's of Bath, but only Fortt's make the Original Bath Oliver Biscuits, as their old maroon and yellow wrappers proclaim on the dis-

tinctive tall cylinders in which they are sold. The true Bath
Oliver is further unique in that each biscuit bears the name and
also a little stamped medallion portrait of its inventor, Dr. William Oliver. These Original Bath Olivers have quite a pedigree.

Dr. Oliver was a notable eighteenth-century physician, a
graduate of Pembroke College, Cambridge, who practised in
Bath at a time when the city was the most fashionable Spa in
England. He cured countless patients who could not afford expensive cures and, being an epicurean as well as a physician,
experimented with food, trying to find a palatable, easily digested,
nutritious biscuit. Thus he originated the Bath Oliver.

Dr. Oliver practised in Bath for thirty years, and there died
in 1764 mourned by rich and poor as one of the kindliest of
benefactors. Before his death, when he knew that soon he would
no longer need the services of his faithful coachman, Atkins, he
set him up in a little bake-shop, gave him some sacks of the finest
wheaten flour, and one hundred pounds sterling. He also gave
him his own recipe for the thin biscuit he had "invented." From
the beginning Atkins' Biscuits were known as Dr. Oliver's Biscuits,
and became popular and fashionable. When Akins died, his shop
and the secret recipe were passed on, first to Norris and to others
in succession, until the recipe was passed to Fortt, whose heirs
still manufacture Dr. Oliver's biscuits made just as the doctor
made them.

After two hundred years, Bath Olivers are still popular, for
they are among the few biscuits that "can logically be served with
every meal," as Fortt's say; they are crisp and tempting, excellent with wine, cheese or butter.

Few among the many distinctive English biscuits have such a
long and well-defined pedigree as the Bath Oliver, and few go so
well with every meal. But many that bear other manufacturers'
names have been household words for more years than I can
count: Carr's, Crawford's, Romary's, Jacob's, and Peak, Frean's,
to mention only a handful. Moreover, like Fortt's of Bath, most
biscuit manufacturers market their goods in the same type of tins,

with the same labels and wrappings, that were as familiar to me as a child at home as the cottage loaf.

Factory-made biscuits did not become generally popular until after the invention of new mixing machinery in the second half of the nineteenth century. About 1865 marked the turning point between the old hardtack and the new easy-to-eat, crumbly biscuits of today. These were smaller and lighter, and more biscuits were sold to the pound, which looked and proved good value. The mass production era of biscuits began.

Peak, Frean is only one of the many British biscuit manufacturers who have celebrated a hundred years of biscuit making. From a humble beginning they have become one of the greatest exporting companies in the biscuit trade, with overseas companies in India, Canada and Australia. Their London packing department has address stencils for every country in the world.

Export for Peak, Frean started in 1860, in hardtack days, with the sale of ships' biscuits to clippers and square-rigged vessels. The "twice-baked" biscuits cascaded from their oven into baskets, were taken to a heated kiln room and finally packed, in sacks for short voyages, and in wooden puncheons for ships trading in the Far East. The following year, household biscuits went to Australia, and it was not long before Peak, Frean biscuits were on sale in most of the important cities of the world, and in the United States since the close of the Civil War.

Bread in the form of biscuits has proved just as important in modern warfare as in mediaeval days. Peak, Frean got their first wide publicity during the Franco-Prussian War of 1871, when Paris was besieged and the people starving. The French government, anticipating the raising of the siege, arranged through the House of Rothschild for ten to eleven million of fine Navy biscuits—nearly five thousand tons—to be made. Peak, Frean's went into day-and-night production and delivered their version of twice-cooked bread to the needy French. Successively they were great Army suppliers during the South African Boer War,

World War I, and World War II, when they provided British troops with, perhaps, their major supplies of all kinds of biscuits, in addition to thousands of their canned Christmas Puddings.

Yet it is not at all as a war-time supplier that the public thinks of Peak, Frean's. Their sweet biscuits have won a place among the best home-made cakes at the tea table, and generations of children have clamored for Pat-a-Cake, Playmate and other lines of their household names in biscuits.

"Pat-a-Cake," the first low-priced biscuit of a shortbread kind, dates from 1902; "Marie" from 1875; "Chocolate Table," the first chocolate-coated biscuit, from 1899; "Bourbon," the first cream sandwich biscuit, from 1910. These are truly old favorites that may be purchased in separate packets or assorted in those long flat tins that Peak, Frean's call P. F. Assorted Biscuits. A biscuit must be good to keep its popularity for fifty years or more both at home and abroad. The firm once had a letter from overseas addressed to them as:

> Messrs. Peek Frean,
> 47, Royal Appointments,
> London

They keep that envelope as a sort of D.S.C., Distinguished Service Order, with forty-seven Royal Appointments, no doubt, their eventual goal in the misty future.

Home-made Bread

7 lbs. of flour
2 qts. of warm water
1 teaspoonful salt
1 gill of yeast

Mix the flour and salt together in a basin, forming a well in the middle. Mix the yeast with warm water, and pour it into the well. Gradually stir the water into the flour until the whole forms into a soft dough. Now knead the dough

well for about 20 minutes; when quite smooth, sift a little
flour over the dough, and cover with a fresh white cloth.
Leave the covered dough to rise in a warm place for about
4 hours. Knead again for ¼ hour. Cover once more, and
let it rise again for about 1 hour.
Divide into 4 loaves. Put these into greased and floured tins
to "prove" for ¼ hour.
Put the "proved" loaves into a quick oven at first, allowing
the oven to cool gradually as the loaves bake.
Bake for about 2 hours.
When baked, the bread should be turned out of its baking
tin on to a sieve, or leaned against a plate to allow it to air.
Properly baked bread should sound hollow when tapped.

A Short-cut Method of Making Bread

½ oz. of yeast to 1 lb. of flour

After mixing and then kneading the dough steadily and
thoroughly so that the bread is free from holes and lumps,
the dough is divided and placed straight away into the
tins and put to rise. In half an hour the dough doubles
its size, and is then ready for placing in the previously
heated gas or electric oven, and baked for about 30
minutes.

Soda or Irish Bread

Yeast is as a rule an ingredient of standard bread. This soda
bread breaks the rule and is yeastless. It is quick and easy
to make, and very good, especially when spread with
butter and honey.

1 heaped teaspoonful of baking soda
1 heaped teaspoonful of salt
¼ teaspoonful of cream of tartar
1½ lbs. of wholemeal flour
1 lb. of ordinary flour
Buttermilk to mix

Unless these ingredients are thoroughly mixed the soda leaves
brown and bitter spots in the bread. With all is well mixed,

moisten with buttermilk (or sour milk will substitute) to
a soft dough, and turn on to a well floured board.

Knead with floured hands for but two or three minutes.

Flatten out the dough to make either one large or four small
loaves about 1½ inches thick.

Bake in a quick oven for about ¾ to 1 hour.

Bread Garnishings

Brown Crumbs—to serve with Game

Shake the breadcrumbs into hot butter in a frying pan, and
toss them about until they are a bright golden brown.

Drain, and spread on absorbent paper in the oven until they
are dry and crisp.

Forcemeat Balls and Veal Stuffing

6 oz. breadcrumbs (¾ cup)

4 oz. butter (or chopped suet)

2 oz. chopped lean bacon

1 egg

*1 teaspoonful each of chopped parsley, thyme, and mixed herbs
and lemon rind*

Season with salt, Cayenne pepper and mace

Form the mixture into balls. Dust with flour and bake in the
dish with the veal.

The amount of stuffing needed to stuff the veal is additional
to the above quantities of the accompanying balls.

Forcemeat balls may also be fried in hot butter.

Sage and Onion Stuffing for pork, goose and duck.

1½ lbs. of onions

1 dessertspoonful mixed sage

3 oz. breadcrumbs

2 teaspoonfuls of salt

½ teaspoonful pepper

Peel and boil the onions a half hour.

Drain them well, and chop them.

Add the sage, breadcrumbs and seasoning, and mix well together.

Stuffing for Poultry

1 pint breadcrumbs

1 teaspoonful pepper

1 small teaspoonful salt

1 oz. thyme and a little chopped parsley

1 egg

Melt a piece of butter, the size of an egg, in a cup of boiling water.

Mix breadcrumb mixture into the liquid and add the egg.

It was enjoyed by Dr. Johnson

14. Ten Cheese Classics

CHEESE, BREAD AND ALE, or wine, are The Ancient Three funda-
mental foods of man. It may be that Arab herdsmen, carrying
ewes' milk stored in a leather bag made from a sheep's stomach,
were the first to find the cheese curds good. However that may
be, cheese was the mainstay of nomadic Asiatic tribes and the
strengthening diet prescribed for Greek athletes training on
Mount Olympus. And, in the Old World, over the centuries, every
nation developed its own characteristic cheese, region by region,
according to the national taste and climate. In England there
has been good bread, good cheese, good beer and good cider
since the days of the first Henry kings, *circa* 1100 A.D.

Cheese, so people say, is one of the best indications of national
character. There are soft and hard cheeses, which Edward
Bunyard further distinguished as the romantics and classics: "The
romantics are apt to run over and become a little offensive when
overripe. Classic cheese do not; age may set them a little more
firmly, but they never give way to it. Pungency and sting they
may and do have, but all within the limits of decency."

In comparing the English epics of Cheshire or Stilton with the
French Camembert, Bunyard concluded that "a Camembert
stands as a sonnet thrown off in a moment of emotion, having
perhaps all the poetic qualities save nobility.* That is as good

* Edward Bunyard, *The Epicure's Companion,* 1937.

195

a summing-up of two national temperaments in terms of cheese as one could wish.

By tradition a pastoral country, England proudly regards her cheeses as among the great achievements of her husbandry. A dozen or so of her "classics" have been in existence since the early Middle Ages; superior by far to the soft rudimentary cheeses made by the nomadic Arabs, they are still made in much the same way as cheese was made when Henry I won the crown by a quick dash to the royal treasury at Winchester.

The Industrial Revolution was well under way before any English cheese was made outside her farmhouses. Not until 1870 was the first English cheese factory opened in Derby. Only slowly did the factory product overhaul the output of farmhouse cheese, and never displaced it until World War II, by wartime edict.

Then, for sixteen bleak years, as epicures mourned, "real" cheese disappeared in Britain. The Government decreed the production of one uniform factory-made cheese, a tasteless imitation of the real thing, soapy enough to be cut up into the minute mousetrap pieces that rationing allowed. In 1954, the lean years over, the ban on locally-made cheese was lifted, making that a great year indeed. The Government, as though to make amends, actually lent a hand to get cheese back to local enterprise where it belonged.

A scheme for the grading and marketing of farmhouse cheese was introduced. Its object was three-fold: to make the production of fine-quality farmhouse cheese an attractive proposition to farmers, to ensure that the cheesemakers' art did not die out, and to restore to English epicures their own top-ranking cheese classics. Thus the old skills, scrupulously handed down from generation to generation of expert cheese-makers, came back into their old high estate. In 1938, or before Hitler, there had been 1,300 farmhouse cheese-makers in England and Wales; in 1957 there were 170

Though the latter number is diminished, it has been off-set

by a four-fold increase in the cheese output of local creameries—
I like the old word "dairies" better. These co-operative cheese-
making centers are run by two or more farmers, who join to
manufacture all of their cheese at one farm. At least 750 of
England's best hotels now regularly serve a full choice of English cheeses, and that choice includes the ten classics, some of
which boast a noble pedigree: Cheddar, Cheshire, and Caerphilly;
Derby, Double Gloucester, and Dorset Blue Vinny; Lancashire,
Leicester, Stilton, and Wensleydale.

After the Industrial Revolution, the varieties of English cheese
took their names from their place of origin rather than from any
particular cheese-maker. Nowadays this is a bit confusing because
the place of a cheese's origin is often some distance from the
place where it is actually made. Cheese-making is largely con-
centrated in the South-West, the West Midlands, and the North-
East. Dorset, in South-West England, contains one of the biggest
cheese-making centers in the world.

One of the ten classics, Cheddar, has become a household
word in four continents. "West of Wells, just under the Mendip
Hills, lies Cheddar," wrote Camden, the historian, in 1588, "famous for its excellent prodigious cheeses made there, some of
which require more than a man's strength to put them on the
table, and of delicate taste." Old Camden's words about size still
hold true, for a whole Cheddar cheese weighs between 65 and 75
pounds; but though Cheddar is still made on West-country farms,
it is also made in other places in England, as well as in Canada,
Australia, New Zealand, South Africa, and the United States.

The reason for Cheddar's popularity is two-fold: firm-bodied,
it withstands the rigors of travel and keeps well. Ready to eat
in three to six months, it is mature and still in perfect order at
nine to ten. Too, Cheddar is versatile; it eats well on its own, and
can be used either as a main or secondary element in a multitude
of dishes. In any company, Cheddar is an excellent mixer.

There is, however, as much difference between a good and an
indifferent Cheddar as there is between a true Burgundy and

a "Burgundy-type" wine. The immigrant Cheddar, which people
are apt to regard chiefly as a mousetrap, "store" or cooking cheese,
is a pale imitation of the cheese that is made in the shadow of
Mendip Hills. True Cheddar is rich, buttery and crumbly, with
a distinctive nutty flavor and a pronounced, sort of Cockney
twang.

Cheshire cheese is hard like Cheddar, but there the likeness
ends. It is no commoner like Cheddar, and its established pedigree
is older. Cheshire men stoutly maintain that their cheese cannot
be made outside Cheshire proper, and actually little is made
outside that fertile home region, since Cheshire cheese is not
easily imitated.

It is the oldest English cheese. Some say it is as old in origin
as the Roman walls of the city of Chester, and it is certain that
it dates at least from the twelfth century. It was much esteemed
in Elizabethan days as a "quick, fat, rich, well tasted cheese"; it
was enjoyed by Dr. Johnson in the eighteenth century in London's famous Fleet Street inn, *The Cheshire Cheese*, and Mrs.
Beeton of Victorian fame reported it to be "known all over Europe
for its rich quality and fine piquant flavour." Today it is a noble
among its peers on the cheese boards in the best British men's
clubs.

Cheshire has been called the most patriotic of English cheeses,
as there are red, white and blue varieties. Best known is the
red, which is actually more orange than red; the color is created
during making by the addition of a pure vegetable dye called
annatto, extracted from the berries of a tropical plant. White
Cheshire, no different in flavor, is produced with no "make-up."
Blue Cheshire used to be simply a profitable happenstance when
a certain type of mould found its way into the cheese while
ripening. Nowadays this can be "managed" by special treatment,
and blue Cheshire commands a much higher price than the red
or the white, and is richer and stronger in flavor.

Each classic cheese has its own story and its own admirers.
Caerphilly is Welsh, a semi-soft cheese that was named after

the Glamorganshire village in Wales. Derby, one of the rarest, is kin to the still rarer Sage Derby, with its green-tinted layers flavored with sage. Dorset Blue Vinny is the hardest of all cheeses to make, its rough rind enclosing a straw-colored and lightly blue-veined crumbly texture. Lancashire, locally known as "Tastie," no doubt from its ancient nickname "Leigh Toaster," is of premier value as a cooking cheese. Leicester is large, round and of a rich orange color like the October hunter's moon.

Then there is Double Gloucester. I do not know how long the men of Gloucester have been making their large, flat, grindstone-shaped Double Gloucester cheese; but more than three hundred years ago, to underscore their common rights and keep the land free for grazing, once a year, on Whit-Monday, they climbed up steep Coopers Hill in Gloucestershire, carrying rounds of their cheese with them. They set a maypole on the summit, and the lads of the district competed with one another in racing down the hill, bowling their cheeses as they went. Now that their native cheese has been restored to them, the old Whit-Monday custom has been revived.

And there is Wensleydale, with its lovely name and honeyed after-taste; old in origin, though not widely known until shortly before World War II, through the centuries Wensleydale has been one of the prides of Yorkshire. Just as a Yorkshireman would no more think of eating roast beef without Yorkshire Pudding, he would disdain apple pie without Wensleydale cheese, for "Apple pie without Wensleydale cheese is like a kiss without a squeeze."

The recipe for Wensleydale was brought to the Yorkshire Dales by Cistercian monks in early Norman times. When their monastries were pillaged during the reign of Henry VIII, the monks fled. Luckily the abbots of Jervaulx Abbey, and maybe others, left the recipe with the local farmers' wives who continued to make the cheese from sheeps' milk until, in the seventeenth century, they changed to using cows' milk. White Wensleydale, the most common, has a velvety texture and when mature, after a month or so, is creamy enough to spread. The Blue variety is stronger in flavor and harder to come by, but it can be found.

Finally, in my pedigree listing of the cheese classics, comes Stilton, the "King of Cheeses" which, like all kings, stands apart in splendid isolation, in a class by itself. Before World War II, Stilton was traditional Christmas fare. It is expensive to make, due to the enormous amount of care that is needed to bring it to perfection; small, as whole cheeses go, weighing about fourteen pounds, it used to be a recognized Christmas present de luxe. A Stilton at Christmastime when I was a girl was almost as important as the Christmas goose. It was then essentially a winter cheese, a part of that typically English after-dinner scene when the ladies withdrew tactfully to the drawing room while the men stayed in the dining room to linger over the Stilton and the port— and the mice, maybe, waited hopefully in the wainscot to get at the cheese crumbs before the servants swept them away. Then made only in late spring and summer, Stilton is now made the year round and can be enjoyed in all seasons, yet it remains the connoisseur's cheese—for the special occasion, not an everyday essential.

A Mrs. Paulet of Wymondham was long supposed to have invented Stilton cheese, marketing it through the landlord of the Bell Inn at Stilton, Huntingdonshire, about 1790. But uncovering of earlier records of the cheese now give the honor to a Mrs. Orton, of Little Dalby, a cheese-maker of 1730. Undoubtedly many hands contributed to the masterpiece—as many do to its making today—in the Midland districts of Melton Mowbray, the Vale of Belvoir, and the Dove Valley. The nearest natural market place was the Bell Inn at Stilton on the Great North Road. Coaching travelers who stopped there gave it its fine reputation, and called it Stilton, though no Stilton cheese was actually made at Stilton.

A prime Stilton comes creamy white and blue veined, open and flaky of texture; its body is soft and slightly moist within its rather wrinkled skin, and is rich, mellow, strong in flavor. As a meal in itself Blue Stilton needs nothing more than some biscuits, butter and the right wines—a brown sherry as a prelude, a port at the last.

There are two royal Do Not commandments to be observed in serving Stilton. Many people assume that the correct method is to spoon or scoop out each portion from a half cheese, leaving a rind, and that port wine or ale poured into the cheese will improve the flavor. Both practices are heresy, say Stilton specialists of Melton Mowbray. *Never* spoon a Stilton, and *never* pour port or anything else into or onto it—the flavor needs no improving.

Only a silver knife should be used with Stilton. If a whole cheese, the oblong cylinder should be halved, and one half stood upright on its flat uncut bottom. Working from the open face, each portion is cut with the knifepoint at center, base at edge, with a down, over and up scooping slice, or as they say in Melton Mowbray, "Cut high, cut low, cut level." Properly cut, not a crumb of Stilton is wasted.

Port wine, or ale as you prefer, are natural complements of this great cheese, but they should be used only as a beverage. And should you be lucky enough to acquire a real Stilton, do not store it in the refrigerator; it keeps best at a constant room temperature not exceeding 58 degrees Fahrenheit, or as it was kept of old in the farmhouse on a low table or a stone floor in the cool larder.

The anomaly of our Tin Can Era is that not only the old farmhouse cheeses, but their bread and ham and cider and an almost endless list of other things that were once the common fare of country folk have become luxuries of the well-to-do. What was once "home-made" and everyday is nowadays the "find" to be cherished as some rare old wine. Even the stalwart Cheddar, the farmhand's meat of yesterday, is today a product for the connoisseur whose taste is sophisticated enough to know and prize the genuine when he meets it.

Aware of this turnabout, the Milk Marketing Board, which is

sponsoring the post-war resurgence of the great old cheeses, has been careful to see that the genuine is clearly so marked. A trademark pyramid of three cheeses over a black background, encircled by a light blue band in which is lettered *Real Farm-house Cheese,* is the official warranty.

The government itself assures you, as the Governor of the Bank of England might assure you over a gilt-edge note, that: "When a cheese is labelled 'Farmhouse,' you may be sure it comes from an English farm, where the grass is rich, and the cows are called by name, and the milk is thick with cream, and the dairy is cool; where the cheesemaking skill is traditional, taught by mother to daughter, mother to daughter."

At least one segment of our vaunted "modern progress" is advancing by returning to yesterday's homely triumphs.

(No recipes are given for cheese making. This is now outside the scope of the average housewife. Recipes for cheese sauce and cheese in savouries are to be found under their respective chapters. Such dishes as cheese souffle, cheese omelette, cheese fondue are European rather than English in origin. Apart from sauces and savouries, the English on the whole prefer their cheese straight, with crackers—as biscuits and cheese.)

A friendly English inn

15. Ale is Beer, Beer is Ale

SITTING AT THE BAR of a friendly English inn with a tankard of ale in your hand, you may see a lot of history in that clear, cool, sparkling pint if you look for it. For brewing ale, or beer, is as old as the baking of bread. Barley, which provides the body and substance of beer is, with wheat, the oldest cultivated grain in Europe.

Both grains had their origins in wild grasses somewhere about the Eastern Mediterranean, and were grown along the Nile when ancient Egypt was young. An unknown time in the long past, wheat, the white corn, became the favorite for bread, barley for ale. Later, the seeds of the wheat corn and the barley corn were carried westward into Europe by early Neolithic people—much as maize, the Americas' corn, was carried by the roving American Indian from South to North America.

Ale was an old drink in England even before the ale-drinking Saxons, the raiding Danes and the invading Romans stepped ashore, but it was the Normans who provided the first stepping stone from the old ale to today's. To each monastery and abbey they built, they added a brewery and brought order and skill to the brewer's art. After the Dissolution of the Monasteries by Henry VIII, it became the common practice for every farmhouse and country inn to brew its own ale, according to tried Norman methods. Not until after the Industrial Revolution did brewing pass to the large-scale brewers' establishments, where brewing

205

still follows the same essential principles practised in the Norman abbot's kitchen.

Ale, in the early days in England, was either common ale made from malted barley, yeast and water, or spiced ale flavored with a number of spices. Ale flavored with hops is comparatively new, and as "hopped" ale it became known as beer to distinguish it from common ale. All English ale is now "hopped," beer and ale mean the same thing, and the word "beer" covers both ale and stout.

The Romans grew the hop as a garden plant, eating the young shoots in spring as we eat asparagus, and it was not until the fourteenth century that hops were used in Europe to flavor beer. The hopped brew reached Tudor England from Flanders, and at first was popularly condemned. Parliament was petitioned against the "wicked weed that would spoil the taste of the drink and endanger the people." Lusty Henry VIII himself feared it might "dry up the body and increase melancholy," and ruled that there should be no hops in English ale.

But that was only a passing incident in the hop's progress. The hop vine flourished best, as it still does, in the rich moist soil of some six English counties where, like most vines in places that they like, it became persistent and hard to suppress. It climbed and twined—the English name hop comes from the Anglo-Saxon hoppan, to climb—and twisted its way into an extraordinary number of far-reaching affairs.

By slow degrees Englishmen came to like the "hopped" sophistication of ale. Even the old word ale, derived from the name of the Viking's drink, was out-paced by the Dutch or German word *bier* or beer for the ale that contained the taste of the bitter catkins of the hop flower. The laws were changed. Not only ale but the landscape became legally "hopped." Hop acreages grew, stretching beyond the Weald of Kent, though as Defoe wrote in his day, Kent is still the Mother of Hop Grounds. Conical oast-houses, where the hops are dried, clustered across the countryside, their white vanes swinging to the wind, and became as characteristic of hop-growing country as the old-time timberyard sawdust burners are characteristic of the American Northwest.

By the end of the eighteenth century hops had come into their own. All ale was "hopped," and the word "beer" embraced both ale and stout. The wicked weed itself, apart from its use in flavoring, was recognized as possessing qualities that would improve the appetite and promote sleep. Brewing became a matter of great enterprise, some British brewers' trade-marks among the most famous in the world, and hop-picking was graduated from a lowly task to a festival that today vies in color and robust gaiety with the grape harvest in the vineyards of Europe.

For many an East End Londoner hop-picking time is *the* annual country outing, as the hop gardens of Kent become their home for three weeks of late summer harvesting. Like the rabble of a Roman holiday, a Cockney throng, family by family, some 40,000 strong, with their pots and pans, pets and prams, often their prized bits of china and a picture or two to dress up the bare huts waiting to house them, streams out of London by special trains, or by road across London Bridge, and pours down into Kent.

Thousands more from the industrial cities of the Midlands trek to the hopyards of western England. And far and wide, west and south, the gypsies in their gaily painted horse-drawn caravans make their way along the country roads, for in August all roads lead to a hop garden.

By day, the pickers strip the vines, filling the brown canvas troughs with the pale flowers—clusters of leafy cones, pale-green washed with gold—that are hurried to the drying kilns, and by nightfall are a sea of hops upon the oast-house floor. By night, the pickers play piano accordions and sing around their bonfires, poach along the hedgerows or raid unguarded orchards for the ripe or unripe fruit until, filled with unaccustomed fresh air and the drowsy aromatic scent of hops, they at last turn in to sleep.

Only in the oast-houses does work still go on, for drying the pale feather-weight hop flowers is a tricky business. In contrast to the clamorous public picking, hop-drying has a privateness about it as, by relays, five-men teams work round the clock throughout the three weeks' picking season. It is warm and quiet and heavily scented inside the circular oast as the men keep their ceaseless, expert vigil. The hops are still green as they lie knee-deep upon the floor with the faint blue smoke of the drying fire rising through them, tended by the old drier, who judges when the hops are dry and cool enough to feed into the "pockets" suspended from the ceiling beneath the upper floor.

Important as the drier and the hops themselves are in brewing, country folk never forget that the barley corn is the real heart of beer. The song of John Barleycorn, malt liquor personified, was already old when Robert Burns wrote of how, despite ploughing and burying, combing with harrows and thrusting clods on his head, the humble John refused to die and grew upright to harvest again. Nowadays, John Barleycorn personifies the innkeeper, but when Burns wrote of him he was the counterpart of Hiawatha's Mondamin, the Indian's immortal corn.

So it is John Barleycorn who today, under the inn-sign of The Plough, the Wheatsheaf, The Royal Hop Pole and the Hop Leaf, who bids you "Drinke and Welcome" as he waits inquiringly to serve you his fare and a tankard of beer. There are four types of beer with a great range of varieties to choose from; pale ale, mild ale, stout, and Burton.

Pale ale, or "bitter," is generally regarded as the best: no less strong than darker beers, it is made from the highest quality malt, and is the driest and most highly hopped beer. Mild ale is the X or XX of the public bar, a draught beer brewed for quick consumption. The "X" markings were originally the Excise officials' crosses made to signify a cask had been examined and graded for duty, but they now serve as brewers' marks to indicate varieties of beer.

Stout is a beer brewed from highly dried, full-flavored malts with a proportion of roasted malt or barley in the grist. The essential difference between ales and stout is in the use of this roasted material, which gives stout its dark color and individual flavor. Burton is a strong ale of the pale type; a darker and more fully flavored draught-beer than the pale ales. Porter, so often mentioned by writers, and prescribed for and loathed by Elizabeth Barrett Browning when she languished in London's Wimpole Street, was a dark beer, betwixt and between ale and stout. Popular with market porters, who gave it the name, porter lost its appeal when the taste for ales heightened and the stouts grew stouter.

Whichever beer you choose at the friendly inn, it will not be served iced, and this is no British idiosyncrasy. Iced drinks are not favored in that cool climate, iced beer least of all. Unlike American or German beers, the products of Britain's 400-odd brewers lose their sparkle and flavor if too cold, and from vat to bar they are guarded against such a calamity. Yet they are not good either if warm; between 50 to 60 degrees Fahrenheit is the ideal temperature for enjoying them.

Many of the great brewers are men of consequence whose family names have become household words. Whitbread's, established in 1742, Worthington's in 1744, Guinness in 1759, and Bass in 1777, constitute the venerable Big Four of Beer. Appropriately, Whitbread's, the oldest, can also claim that Samuel Whitbread I, its founder, was the all-time dominant personality among Britain's brewers.

Whitbread was an outstanding figure in the London of his day, contemporary with George II and George III, of Alexander Pope and Dr. Johnson, of Gainsborough and Sir Joshua Reynolds, who painted a handsome portrait of him. He was a staunch Parliamentarian, represented his native Bedford in Parliament for an unbroken period of twenty-two years, and was the first man to bring the slave trade to public attention in the Commons.

Whatever Samuel Whitbread I did, he did well. When he built his London brewery by an old and choice well in Chiswell Street, he called in the leading experts of the day: John Smeaton, designer of the Eddystone Lighthouse, to design the underground storage cisterns; James Watt, inventor of the Watt steam engine, and George Rennie, builder of London and Waterloo Bridges, to design and install "a stupendous steam engine" that was one of the wonders of contemporary London, and is now a museum piece in Sydney, Australia.

Samuel Whitbread I lived long enough to see that "from a very small beginning and by great assiduity" he had established an industry destined for greatness. As to the increased output of beer during his own lifetime, he believed "There never was the like before, nor probably ever will be again." However, Whitbread's present Chairman, old Samuel's great-great-grandson, has seen Whitbread's beer carried by the latest ship and airliner, and by transports older than the wheel—sampan, junk and felucca, elephant, camel and bullock—to Egypt, India, Ceylon, China, Malay, and most other inhabited parts of the earth.

Say Guinness and you say stout, which is precisely as the first Arthur Guinness intended it should be. He was an Irishman of one purpose: to brew a good stout and nothing else, using "no unnatural aids to colour or flavour." For that purpose he leased, in 1759, a brewery at St. James's Gate, Dublin for a term of 9,000 years.

By the end of its first hundred years, Guinness was sufficiently established as a stout to have become one of Britain's traditional drinks. It was made a feature of an illustration for Dickens' *Pickwick Papers*. Happy travelers began finding it as far from home as Russia, Turkestan, and Brazil. At the outset of its third century, the stout which bears the trade-mark of the Irish harp, and the slogan "Guinness is Good for you," is still made as its founder ordained, and Guinness still brews only one drink.

In the brewing of any fine beer the quality of the water is as important as that of the barley and hops; it must be the right "brewer's water," and with just such water the thriving com-

munity of Burton-on-Trent is blessed. Out of the blessing grew
Burton ale.

Burton was famous for its ale as early as the time of Richard
Coeur de Lion, as readers of Sir Walter Scott's *Ivanhoe* may
recall. History testifies that, in 1580, beer from the Monks' Brew
House in Burton Abbey was served to Mary, Queen of Scots,
when she was a prisoner hard by in Tutbury Castle. But the year
to which modern Burton points with most gusto is 1777, when
William Bass brewed his first ale using water from a Burton well.

Failure to recognize the name of Bass today is at once a con-
fession that one does not know ale, and that holds true not in
Britain alone but in forty-four countries, wherever ale is quaffed.
Specifically, Bass usually means India Pale Ale. Many others—
Worthington's, who boast three Royal Warrants, Allsopp's, Wat-
ney's of London, to name but a few—have risen to fame in Britain
in the wake of their pale ales, but Bass has ascended to the throne
of the British pale-ale empire.

Why India Pale Ale rather than Burton Pale Ale is a curious
story. Even before 1777 England's ales had followed her empire
builders to India and the Far East, and Hodgson's India Pale
Ale, made in London, was the standard drink of the Englishman
in Calcutta and Bombay. Burton's ales, by an odd quirk, were
far better known in St. Petersburg, Warsaw, and Helsinki; indeed, the Russians thought more of them than did Londoners,
for the reason that little Burton ale went to London. It was
cheaper to ship it by canal and river boats to Hull on the English
coast, and thence by sail ship to the Baltic Sea ports, than it was
to cart it 127 miles to Britain's capital.

Russia, however, resented the growing competition of Burton
ale with vodka, and raised a prohibitive tariff to check the in-
vader. The tariff was a blow to the Bass brewery, which by then
had captured much of the Baltic trade. But most opportunely
the powerful East India Company had some difficulty with its
London brewer of India Pale Ale, and Bass was asked to try

his hand at brewing an ale suitable for India's hot climate. He produced East India Pale Ale, a lighter ale than the old, and it was welcomed joyously throughout India.

In 1827, a shipload of Bass's new ale never reached India, being wrecked in the Irish Channel. The underwriters managed to salvage some of the casks, and sold them for cash in Liverpool. So popular in Liverpool was this ale intended for India that Bass had no choice except to admit Liverpool to his sales territory.

The next Bass in line, a son of William, extended the market further to Northwest England and Ireland, with the result that Bass had to enlarge vastly its brewery. Not until 1851, however, and the succession of a grandson, Michael Thomas Bass, to the ownership, did Bass venture to introduce the ale, long famous in India, to London. It captured London as it had taken Liverpool, by popular surrender.

Michael Thomas Bass was elected to Parliament, and raised to the peerage, becoming Baron Burton. A liberal man, he admitted two of his associates to the Bass ownership, and the company became Bass, Ratcliff & Gretton, Ltd. As such, it is today's premier brewer of India Pale Ale, and a Gibraltar of the British brewing trade.

Fully to enjoy Britain's best brews, one should have some knowledge of their labels. Those of the old-timers are as colorful and carefully designed as any armorial bearings, and were shipping marks before the Trade Marks Registration Act became a law in 1875. Often they convey special meanings to the connoisseur.

For example, the Bass Red Triangle, adopted as a mark in 1850, stands on the registry as Trade Mark No. 1, and identifies the original India Pale Ale. It was immortalized by Monet, the French impressionist, in his painting *Bar aux Folies Bergère*. The Red Triangle bears the message to the knowing that the ale was left to mature finally in its bottle, and should be "rested" a few days before serving in order to allow the last bit of sediment to settle.

The Bass Blue Triangle marks a similar pale ale for which no "resting" is required, as it was aged wholly in the cask, and at once pours clear and sparkling.

Trade Mark No. 2 on the registry is the Bass Diamond; in several colors, it marks as many different mild ales and stout. In all, Bass uses twelve labels each with a meaning of its own.

So with the marks of Whitbread and Worthington; the Irish Harp of Guinness alone means but one thing: the same "good old stout" brewed with "malt and hops, without any mixture of unwholesome material whatever." The only material changes that today's science and mechanization claim for any the great traditional brews is the production of more of them, plus a consistency of quality that the old farmhouse brewers, devoted to rule-of-thumb methods, could not always guarantee.

Britons cling to no hard and fast rules as to when to serve beer or to whom. In the main, it is regarded as a man's drink, though I am one woman who knows no greater delight than a glass of cool ale on a summer evening at one of England's old country inns. By and large, it is the people's drink; the chief spot to find it is at the "pub," but as Worthington's royal warrants testify, it may also be found in the best places. You will find it on the hunt, at the races, and in London's finest clubs, but most of all you will find it relished at the workaday lunch. In England, a man may be gloriously, if quietly, content with himself, his job, the government, and the world, if at noontime, as he will, he may settle down to a crust of honest bread, real farmhouse cheese, and a pint of true British ale.

And as he sits and munches and sips, he may reflect that this land of his, though bomb-scarred, never had to endure so harrowing an experience as Prohibition; and he may even recall old John Taylor's tribute to good ale. John Taylor (1580-1633) once sailed a boat of brown paper on the Thames, was a collector of revenue on wines, and was known for his writings as The Water Poet. In *Drinke and Welcome* he saw ale as an emblem of justice:

"... for it allows and yields measure; it will put courage into a coward and make him swagger and fight; it is a seale to many a goode bargaine; the physician will commend it; the lawyer will defend it; it neither hurts nor kills any but those who abuse it unmeasurably and beyond bearing; it doth good to as many as take it rightly; it is as good as a paire of spectacles to clear the eyesight of an old parish clarke; and, in conclusion, it is such a nourisher of mankinde, that if my mouthe were as bigge as Bishopgate, my pen as long as a may-pole, and my inke a flowing spring or a standing fish-pond, yet I could not, with mouth, pen, or inke, speake or write the true worthinesse of ale."

I hasten to add, inasmuch as my next chapter is on cider, that John Taylor was *not* a West Countryman.

Old cider, old cider

16. Brave Old Cider

"When God had made the oak trees,
And the beeches and the pines,
And the flowers and the grasses,
And the tendrils of the vines;
He saw that there was wanting
A something in His plan,
And He made the little apples
The little cider apples,
The sharp, sour cider apples,
To prove His love for man." *

WHO WROTE THAT DITTY I do not know, but he must have
been a West-countryman, and I like to think that he was from
Herefordshire. Cider is England's ancient wine, and the county
of my birth was famous for its cider long before Hereford cattle
gave it the double cattle-cider crown. Today it probably produces
as much cider as the rest of England put together.

To the Herefordshire farmhand of my memory, surely something vital would have been missing if cider had not been at hand.
And it always was. Cider strengthened his labor, cheered his
leisure, blessed all his endeavors.

When the calendar was still pinpointed with folk-lore days,

* Was it G. K. Chesterton, London-born, who loved "the apple wine of
Hereford" and the road?
"Where the apple wood of Hereford
Goes all the way to Wales"

The Blessing of the Wheat—a virtual baptism of the young winter-sown wheat in old cider—was the first event of every Hereford-shire New Year. And hanging from the center of the raftered ceiling at Ladye Grove was the symbol of this ancient custom, a strange blackened oval of twisted hawthorn twigs, known as the "bush." In my time the "bush" was a country bygone, but that suspended from a rafter had been preserved from the old days at The Hyde, and I believe it was the very last of its kind.

The Blessing of the Wheat took place, in slightly differing forms, in the dark cold hours of the early morning of New Year's Day, or on some farms on the eve of Twelfth Night. Perhaps be-cause of the surfeit of Christmas fare and the long work to prepare it, the ceremony was a rite rather than a feast or festival.

At The Hyde, my mother recalls, the men, dressed in the clean white smocks that they ordinarily wore on Sundays, took lanterns lighted with tallow candles and started out soon after 5 o'clock on New Year's Day, with my grandfather leading the way. Fires were lit in one of the wheatfields, already a tender green with young wheat; a freshly cut branch of hawthorn was twisted into shape over the flames, and old cider was sprinkled on the ground. The lanterns swayed to and fro like incense-burners as the bless-ing was chanted three times. Then cider was drunk around the fires to a chorus of OLD CIDER, OLD CIDER, BRAVE OLD CIDER, HURRAH! There was a time when farm answered farm in the cider chant, so that it seemed that all Herefordshire was hallooing.

By Twelfth Night Eve, in farmhouse after farmhouse, the old hawthorn bush was taken down, and the new one hung from the kitchen ceiling. No one would dare, for it would be courting the Devil, to take down the bush between one Twelfth Night and the next. Though I am sure God-fearing Herefordshire folk would not admit it, the bush was a lone surviving spirit of the store room from among the lares and penates, those household gods of hearth and home that had been worshipped in Roman times.

Hanging where all could see it, the bush bore testimony that the ceremony of the wheat's blessing, without which the crops would not grow, had been faithfully carried out. It served to protect the house from fire and lightning throughout the year. Pagan maybe it was, but it betokened a God-fearing respect for bread and cider, the staple diet of the old Herefordshire farm-hand.

He both breakfasted and supped on toast and hot cider, spiced with rosemary and sugar. Cider was his noon-time reviver, provided as part of his regular wage, and he carried it to the fields in an oaken keg, or harvest bottle, his initials often branded deep in the hand-polished wood. At dusk he would go home, tired but content, to find the loaves and cups of cider set. Those were the days, as my elders say with a wise shake of the head, when bread and cider were real.

Even as beer and wine, cider is one of the oldest of fermented drinks, and Englishmen once drank it—thousands still do—in preference to ale. Its partisans say that cider made from the juice of ripe cider-making apples is the most wholesome of all drinks; that habitual cider-drinkers are immune against gout, gravel and stone, that it relieves sufferers from rheumatism, and is a digestive aid. At the time of the Black Death when a quarter of England's population was wiped out, not a single case of Asiatic cholera was reported in Herefordshire, thanks to cider if you believe the old tales.

To cider is attributed why Herefordshire men and women so often live, alert and apple-cheeked, to remarkably old ages. The classic example is cited of the group of Herefordsire elders who danced a Morris dance and made music as after-dinner entertainment to King James on one of his royal visits. The four musicians each averaged 106 years of age, the twelve dancers more than 100. These devotees of Brave Old Cider had been born in the reign of Henry VIII, lived through the great Elizabethan Age, and survived hale and hearty to play and dance before a Stuart king.

The quality of cider depends naturally enough upon the quality of the cider-making apples, which are as different from table apples as wine grapes are from table grapes. Cider, of a sort, can be made from an assortment of apples, windfalls or otherwise, and a passably fair cider can be made from a few exceptional kinds of table apples; but really fine cider can only be made from special vintage cider apples, the very best from a careful blend of sharps and bittersweets—small, harsh and astringent, highly-colored bright and beautiful apples.

The art of making fine cider is simple when the best varieties of fruit, grown in the right soil, and in a perfect state of maturity, can be obtained. Simple, that is, by the old method—primitive it might be called now—when quality was as important as quantity, and a man could say with surety whether the apples used were Foxwhelps, Redstreaks or Styres.

First the windfalls would be gathered, then the bulk of the fruit, which fully ripened falls naturally to the ground, and lastly a late picking of the remainder, which was often shaken from the trees by long poles each with a hook at the end. The fruit was then left in heaps to mellow in the open air before being carted to the mill.

The mill of generations of cider makers in all cider-making counties of England and in northern France consisted of the "runner" or stone wheel, somewhat in the shape of a flour mill-stone, running on its edge in the "chace" or circular stone trough. Horse-driven, or rather horse-plodded, the weight of the slowly revolving stone-runner reduced the fruit to pulp. The expressed juice was then put into casks to ferment; as soon as possible it was separated from the grosser lees, and drawn off from one cask to another to prevent excessive fermentation. When the old English codlin apple was abundant in Herefordshire, cider made from that apple was ready to drink by Michaelmas, and was sometimes made purposely to be drunk in the harvest of the same year. The old cider-makers, however, kept their best cider two years in the cask before bottling, or until the spring twelve-month after making. The alcoholic content of cider so aged is rarely more than seven per cent, which makes it far milder than most wines.

Nowadays the old stone mills have been promoted, or downgraded, according to your view, to ornamental features in a garden or to farmyard curiosities. Together with the traveling cider mills that succeeded them, they are relics of the past, bygones like the harvest bottle and the hawthorn bush, and the fruit now goes in bulk by motorized horsepower to the cider-making factories with their huge vats and mechanized equipment. Thus onward has marched the art.

Yet there was merit in the old stone mill. Thomas Andrew Knight, a famous horticulturist of his day, and a man who probably knew more about the virtues of vintage cider-apples than anyone else, declared in 1801 that the stone mill, "This engine," as he called it, "is not without its imperfections; but it is the best that has yet been, and perhaps, taking its merits in the aggregate, the best that ever will be invented." He continued: "I am convinced that Herefordshire has derived no small portion of its fame as the cider country from the judicious use of its mill." He might have added that the stone mill was simple and enduring, seldom got out of order, and then was easily repaired. An old horse could work it without tiring, and small quantities of fruit could be ground as they became available, to produce "stout-bodied, rough, masculine cider." *

Little Harry, as we called him, gave me my first taste of cider. He was a small puckish man who said you could always keep dry in the rain if you dodged the raindrops, and who dared to climb the highest elm trees, like a steeplejack, and bring down the coveted eggs from a crow's nest. The cider he gave me in secret, under the high-pitched shadowed roof of the barn, was, I do not doubt, rough, masculine cider. He laughed as I puckered my face and handed back the horn mug that was the farmhands' traditional drinking cup. I never appreciated my true native drink, a

* Mary Roberts, *Annals of My Village*, 1831.

fine rich full-flavored cider, until long after Little Harry had "gone to the war." He never came back.

In my own home, cider was ordinarily draught cider drawn fresh from the cask, a wooden peg in the bunghold, in the cool cellar where it was kept, and it was served in a cider pitcher. It is better kept this way when the demand is constant, and our noon-time lunch was no lunch to my father without that cool, straw-colored drink. But the qualities of cider are volatile and escape if exposed to the air, and the prime brands of cider, for high days and holidays, were kept in straw-encased bottles lying on their side in the cellar wine bin, a cobwebbed stack of dark square pigeonholes. Good cider not only improves in the bottle for a certain period but will keep almost any length of time, fifty years or more.

Perry, made from the fermentation of the juice of ripe perry-making pears, is cider's west-country rival, though cider has the greater fame and long since has eclipsed perry in popularity. But many a Herefordshire man has come, in the long run, to prefer perry as his regular drink.

The rules and methods of making fine cider are identically true of fine perry. Of the two, perry is lighter in color, less stout-bodied, less rough perhaps than cider. Indeed, a fine perry (and this was true by repute of perry made from the pear, Taynton Squash, which was what the Foxwhelp was among apples, first and best), is of a quality little inferior to the best champagne. And a light perry, containing up to four per cent alcohol and aged to dryness so as to have lost almost all its sweetness while preserving its flavor and astringency, resembles the light sauterne *Vin de Grave,* and is excellent with fish and meat.

Perry is also a fine blender. Some good judges of wine prefer a blend of perry and cider to drinking either one straight. And there was a shrewd suspicion in the old days that wine merchants increased their profits by adding perry to wine. Andrew Knight, the expert quoted earlier, maintained that perry made from a once-famous vintage pear, the Barland, when blended judiciously with port wine defied detection.

The yield of perry encouraged blending. Pear trees live much longer than apple trees and grow to a larger size, in height rather than in breadth. A pear tree fully grown is the aristocrat of fruit trees, approaching in grandeur and ornamental appearance the oaks and elms of some ancestral park. Once the pear was a pillar of the Herefordshire landscape, and a few old stagers are still left. I recall an orchard of them just below Ladye Grove, relics of an age that closely obeyed the principles of good planting, the trees being set 40 feet apart—apples were spaced only a few feet less.

The native wines of those bygone orchards could, in their heyday, compete with the most famous grape wines of Europe. John Evelyn records in 1664 how a Herefordshire squire wagered a London vintner that he could produce a cider that would excel his best Spanish or French wine. A trial of the wines took place before different judges on three separate occasions. Each time the verdict was in favor of cider—BRAVE OLD CIDER!

Why, you may ask, if cider is so good, has beer risen to the tree-wine's once proud place as the Englishman's most favored drink? The answer goes back to the Napoleonic Wars when the price of grain and meat rose enormously and farmers, turning their attention to the more profitable crops, grubbed up their orchards. Vintage fruit became scarce, good cider was thinned with water to make five hogsheads out of three, and in time— outside the cider-producing counties—the public lost the taste for good cider and fine perry, and the old tree-wines of England never regained their full trade.

Today, though beer has outpaced cider consumption in England threefold, cider is still very much an Englishman's drink; upwards of 20,000,000 gallons of it, sweet or dry, sparkling or still, are bottled or on draught yearly.

Brave Old Cider! So Rex Harrison, after the first-night opening show of *My Fair Lady* in London, must have said. The American magazine *Life* pictured his wife, Kay Kendall, bringing supper backstage to him after that night's smashing success: hot sausages, and bottles of cider. Quaffing it down he might have coined the critics' cheer of the evening's performance, not fair but fabulous. For today's fine vintage cider is as good, according to its partisans, as any that Herefordshire's squires of old so heartily applauded, though the names of such vintage cider apples as Foxwhelp and Redstreak have been replaced by Breakwell's Seedling, Sweet Coppin, and Yarlington Mill.

Bulmer's of Hereford are the largest cider-makers in the world. In 1887, the year of Queen Victoria's Jubilee, Mr. Bulmer of Hereford city was making his first cider in a wooden shed. Now the firm is "Purveyors of Cider by Royal Warrant to The Queen," and maintains standard vats, of Herefordshire oak, with a capacity of 60,000 gallons. Additionally, reinforced concrete vats, especially lined, are used; the largest of these, recently installed, holds 550,000 gallons of cider. Bulmer's boasts that this is one of the largest, if not the largest container in existence for any alcoholic drink.

"Penny-plain" or "twopence-colored," so you may take your choice of cider: casked or bottled; sweet, medium or dry. But do not, the moment your bottle is opened, hasten to drink it so as not to lose any of the briskness. Instead, follow the time-tested way of the wise cider-drinker who likes to see the liquor "cream" in the tankard, and waits until most of the gas has escaped before he drinks. Copy him and the effervescence will not rob you of the true flavor, which should be fine, rich and full.

The Bulmer range, as it is called, includes the Champagne ciders, the standard bottled varieties of cider and perry, and draught cider. Pomagne, the Champagne Cider-de-Luxe, comes in champagne bottles, each bearing its vintage date, and is made from apples exactly the same way as champagne is made from grapes. So with Godwin Champagne Perry, a "baby bottle" of which fills a champagne glass. "Still" cider, once a cure-all by old wives' tales, and too dry for normal palates, is now recommended by the medical profession for rheumatism and diabetes.

Cider is not limited in company to any one food. Like the *vin ordinaire* of France it "goes" with almost everything. And, like wine, good cider can give just that extra fillip to certain cooked meats and fish.

There is, however, a certain affinity between cider and ham. Cold ham and a tankard of cider; a sugar-cured ham boiled in allspice, brown sugar and cider; and a plain salted ham boiled in herbs, peppercorns, sugar and black treacle and sour cider, are all country ways of blending cider and ham. White fish or salmon are also delicious when cooked in dry cider, either baked in the oven or poached in half quantities of cider and water; and half a pint of cider is a good addition to a casserole of chicken.

Old Herefordshire Cider Cake

8 oz. of flour   2 eggs
4 oz. of sugar   ½ grated nutmeg
¼ lb. of butter   1 teacupful of cider
                              1 level teaspoonful bicarbonate of soda

Beat the butter and sugar to a cream.
Add the eggs, well beaten, then the 4 oz. of flour sifted with the bicarbonate of soda and nutmeg.
Pour over all the cider, beaten to a froth. Mix thoroughly.
Stir in remainder of the flour and mix well together.
Bake in a shallow, well-greased tin, for 45 minutes in a moderate oven.

Cider Cup

A bottle of cider
A bottle of soda water
A liqueur glass of brandy
A dessertspoonful of lemon juice
Sugar to taste, and add a few thin strips of lemon rind

Bulmer's Pomagne Cup

One bottle Pomagne champagne cider
2 sherry glasses of sherry
2 sherry glasses of orange squash
Soda water as required

A good addition is the outer skin of a orange or lemon in a wine glass just covered with gin. All to stand for 10 minutes. Pour into the pitcher, and add the other ingredients.

Bulmer's Pomagne Cocktail

This consists of one part Pomagne champagne cider, one part of gin and one part of orange squash.

Bulmer's Pomagne "Special" is similar to the "Special" at The Hyde:

A bottle of Pomagne champagne cider
A wine glass of brandy
A wine glass of Curacao
Slices of orange—and, of course, ice

The era of the tin can had begun

17. Glorifying the Tin Can

ABOUT 1812 two Englishmen, Bryan Donkin and John Hall, hammered out a pot made of sheet-iron coated with tin which they called a "tin canister." They filled it to the brim with a steaming stew of beef, sealed the pot with an iron lid, and then set out to interest the army and navy in their new food-preserving invention.

The era of the Tin Can had begun.

The invention was not wholly original with Donkin and Hall. A year or two earlier Nicholas Appert, a Frenchman, had produced what was to prove to be the most revolutionary cookbook ever written, entitled *The Art of Preserving all Animal and Vegetable Substances for Many Years*. The great Napoleon had inspired the book by appealing to France, a nation of cooks, to devise a preserved ration other than salt pork or beef for his army and navy.

The art of war had advanced to where armies were too large to be fed by raiding the countryside; the crews of far-sailing ships, after months of hardtack and salt fare, were coming down with scurvy. How better to preserve food had become a problem of conquest and empire.

Monsieur Appert's answer was the glass jar, and a way to "can" food that today is known to every housewife. Its flaw, of course, was that glass jars are not wholly safe when entrusted to the care of army teamsters, which was why Donkin and Hall rose to the

229

need. Their tin-coated iron canister was tough enough to ride the roughest roads; it could be opened with no less than a hammer and a chisel, and the easiest way was with an ax, as British army cooks soon learned.

The Duke of Wellington, then Lord Wellesley, himself wrote Donkin and Hall in praise of their new "preserved beef." The Arctic explorer, John Ross, took enough tinned meat and soup with him in search of the Northwest Passage to allow each man of his crew a pound of each a week, and the dreaded scurvy was held at bay. By 1819, the tin can had won such renown at sea that another explorer of North America's Far North, Sir Edward Parry, took with him not only tinned meat and soup but 10,000 pounds of tinned carrots; the shades of that expedition might well groan in memory.

History seems to have made no note of it, but I have not the least doubt that canisters of good English beef had an honored place about the campfires of the Iron Duke on the eve of Waterloo, and so marked a double triumph for England. At any rate, for war, the glass jar passed with Napoleon, and the tin can became as essential to armies as hobnailed boots. The British troops who guarded the fallen Emperor at St. Helena subsisted on tinned beef.

However, iron canisters that were best opened with an ax did not fit well into the home scheme, and the French-devised glass jar did. So that while Napoleon lost Waterloo he must be credited with introducing "home-canned" foods to the English fireside. I pause to wonder which victory was greater, the glass jar's or Wellington's?

And I wonder over another singular fact: that the sword has had much more to do with shaping the mold of modern England's traditional fare than has either the peeling knife or the carving knife. First the Saxons changed the cooking of the Celts, next the Romans added their notions to the Saxons', and finally the Norman Conquest brought a refinement and civility to every phase of Anglo-Saxon life.

Finally? No, not even the Normans furnished the last word. The New World was discovered, and the best of the American Indian's fare became England's too. Britons moved with the flag into India, and in time back to the homeland came curry, Worcestershire Sauce and other English traditionals of today.

Then, the glass jar!

From caveman days, cooks had been trying to devise ways to preserve food through the winter and the hungry times of drought and famine. Hunters smoked and salted their meats, fishermen dried their catch in the sun, salted or packed fish in oil; farm wives made cheese from milk, and dried the fruit for keeping. Why nobody thought of the glass jar and tin can until as late as the nineteenth century is an unanswered indictment of human ingenuity.

One need not have many gray hairs to remember "canning time" in the country, or "bottling time" as they say in England. Jars by the scores, glass lids and caps of metal, the black or red rubber bands for sealing, thermometers, were all part of the paraphernalia that surrounded the cooking in the great wide copper preserving pans of my old home. Wooden spoons for stirring were indispensables.

The preserving season started properly towards the end of January and February when it was lemon curd and marmalade-making time; the putting up of fruit in glass began around Whitsuntide, fifty days after Easter, when the gooseberries were hard and green and sour, and little bigger than green peas. Then there was a lull until the bottling-fruit-and-jam season got under way, first with the raspberries and strawberries of June, and the black-currants of July. But that was merely a prelude to the mid-August-through-to-mid-September frenzy of coping with the putting up of pears, damson and greengages, and the commoner sorts of plums.

Everything was subordinated to the business in hand. Little patience was shown to any children, dogs or cats who got underfoot, though "good" children were allowed to lick the spoons.

And to make matters more exciting the windows and doors were kept closed to deter enemy wasps; while on filling the jars there was always a possibility of one of them cracking, a hazard that seemed a perilous affair. But when all was done, when the sticky pots and long-handled spoons were put away, and the bottles and jars sealed down, there came that moment of supreme satisfaction. The store-cupboard revealed a multi-colored country hoard: row on row of summer splendour in the cardinal red of currants, the royal purple of damsons, the green and gold of gooseberry and greengage plums. Many a time later my mother must have paused as she took some preserve or other from a shelf, to look with quiet satisfaction at the harvest she had so faithfully gathered in. Here was wealth!

Home cooks who can forget aching feet and long hours over a hot stove, and find only joy in well-filled shelves of their very own, will always "put up" something, just as a dauntless Old Guard will always bake its own bread. But even in Britain's most smiling countryside today, home bottling or canning with its toils and rewards seems destined to go the way of the grain cradle and the plough-horse. Factory "put up" food has also become a tradition.

A rather proud one, too, with its museums of rare old pots, jugs and other tools, its venerable history, its scrupulous preservation of some of the best of the old-home recipes, and some additions of its own that are now as revered as the famous old *Cheshire Cheese* inn off the Strand. No company in Britain has done more to bring honor to the tin can in the land of its birth than has the London firm of Crosse & Blackwell, Ltd.

These grocers to the world date their origin to 1706, in the reign of Queen Anne, when two "oilmen" and "salters" began trading in London's Soho, specializing in pickles, sauces and condiments. Then operating as West & Wyatt, the firm sold mainly to the nobility and wealthier gentry. That preference was not begotten of snobbishness, but reality. Ordinary folk who relished pickles and like luxuries put up their own or went without. And so a century droned into a second.

In 1829, Mr. William Wyatt intimated that he wished to retire, and no new West or Wyatt was in sight to carry on the family business. Two brash young employees, Edmund Crosse and Thomas Blackwell, stepped into the breach. Each was 25 and had served his apprenticeship under Mr. Wyatt. Their one difficulty was in raising £600, the price that old Mr. Wyatt asked for his little establishment.

Family farmsteads were sold, other money borrowed from relatives, who parted with it most reluctantly, and in 1830 Crosse and Blackwell took possession. They lived over the tiny plant to save paying rent elsewhere, put their profits back into the enterprise, and in 1839 they opened a retail shop on Soho Square. That address has since become the company's world headquarters, largely because of the young founders' devotion to Appert's epochal discovery and the invention of the tin-coated iron canister by Donkin and Hall.

Crosse and Blackwell set out to glorify the container as much as its contents, to make the most of their radical use of individualistic jars, pots and cans in place of the old serve-all bins, barrels and tubs. They sought the services of London's greatest chefs, among them Alexis Soyer of the Reform Club; Charles Francatelli, later lured away to become chef to Queen Victoria; and the famous Qualiotti who invented piccalilli. The partnership was on so solid a foundation by 1864 that it absorbed the canister business of Donkin and Hall.

That absorption, however, was strictly on the plebeian side of the ledger, by way of securing the firm's bulk trade with army messes at home and abroad, and the provisioning of ships at sea. It was the carriage trade, which soon included the Royal Family and the brightest peers of the realm, that commanded the firm's main attention, and only the very best that the rising new packaging indusry could contrive in containers was allowed to convey a Crosse & Blackwell preserved food to the customer.

An exhibit of wares at the Universal Exhibition at Vienna in July 1873 inspired the *Deutsche Zeitung* to report in its review of the preserved foods division of the fair:

"The largest firm in the world in this branch is Crosse and Blackwell, of London, who show an astonishing collection of Preserves in tins and boxes, mostly articles of luxury, which excel not only by the well-known quality of their contents, but, in many instances, also by their handsome and costly exterior, so artistically designed and in many instances of the finest Wedgwood porcelain. One would almost think, if the contrary were not so well known, that the vases and not the contents were the first consideration with that house and the most has been made of this opportunity to show them off to the best advantage."

During those decades of glorifying porcelain "vases" that preceded today's humble and ubiquitous tin can, no representative of Crosse & Blackwell set foot inside a customer's door unless properly attired in tail coat and top hat, gloves and stick. Not until World War I had brought Britain's lean years was a salesman permitted to wear a plain business suit and bowler hat when on duty.

Perhaps it is as well that the tail coat and top hat did vanish with Sarajevo in 1914, for by then the knell of the Wedgwood container as the symbol of factory "put up" food had been rung too. About 1900 the machine took over the manufacturing of tin cans, the can as we know it emerged, and around it after the war's end developed a remarkable phenomenon.

So overwhelming is this phenomenon today that one is left breathless by trying to grasp its magnitude, but there it is! Tin cans, literally billions of them turned out by a multitude of great food-processing factories, now provide no small portion of every family's fare in Britain, America and much of the world. It is the home-made dishes of yesterday's farmhouse kitchens that have become the luxuries of the noble and rich!

The past Christmas my husband and I, together with many

thousands of others who would be flattered to be classed among the carriage trade, sat down to a Christmas pudding from a Crosse & Blackwell tin can, a can that, once cut open, was of so little value it is now rusting on the town dump. Yet that tin brought us a pudding such as Queen Victoria once ate—it was almost as good as the Christmas pudding of my old home!

The Duke of Wellington himself

I can imagine the brows of the Crosse & Blackwell management lifting in pained surprise at my qualifying *almost,* but it stands unabashed. I am happy to grant that the reputable factory may give its canned foods a uniformity in quality that no home cook can surpass and few can equal; that tinned and quick-frozen foods have created a kitchen-free liberty so abundant that it is often a problem what to do with all of it. Thanks to mass production's robot canners, wholesome fare has been put within the means of everybody, and all of us are probably richer in vitamins than were our mothers and grandmothers.

All glory to the tin can!

But what wanderer away from his homeland pines for that good old tinned pudding the local grocer kept on his shelf? What soldier dreaming of home craves the good things from the tins that Mother warmed up so well?

Full of vitamins the products of the robot canners may well be, scrupulously sanitary the cooking vats of the factory, yet something is missing from even the best that the great food processors have to sell. Perhaps it is absence of the touch that goes indefinably with love of a task well done by one's own hands; perhaps it is lack of that intuitive wisdom with which all truly good cooks of my native countryside seem to have been born, and which is common to good cooks the world over. Or perhaps, and I think this is the nub, the tin can at most can hold only a good reproduction of the "real thing," that it is as the printed picture is to the painted masterpiece.

No matter how fine the print, the original alone conveys the full warmth and genius of the artist who created it, putting something of himself on his canvas. Time is a great winnower. After a while we are apt to tire of reproductions, and prefer to hang an original on the wall.

That is what is happening in England today, as the forty lean years dwindle into memory. Once more the old masterpieces of the kitchen, the *real* fare of Englishmen, are returning to vogue both in homes and good public eating places. Wherever time and care are still counted as ingredients of the dish, and a zest for doing-it-yourself prevails, the old-time favorites are again being prepared, and they savor of the best acclaimed by gourmets of a century and a half ago.

The wheels of change have come a full cycle for the English roadside inns. Robbed by the railways of their stage-coach patronage, the automobile has given them back that lost trade with interest compounded. Innkeepers once more are finding it worth their while to be guided by the traditional cookbooks that brought food-fame to their ancestors and their region.

For unlike the masterpieces of art, which belong only to museums and to an elite few, the masterpieces of the kitchen can be recreated over and over. The secret lies simply in doing in one's own kitchen what all good artists do in their studios—of putting something of one's self into the pot, and thrilling to the joy that alone can bring.

INDEX TO RECIPES

Index to Recipes

BREAD, HOME-MADE
189

BREAD SAUCE
117

BREAD, SHORTCUT METHOD
190

BROWN CRUMBS
191

BROWN FOUNDATION SAUCE
119

BROWN MEAT GRAVY
118

BULMER'S POMAGNE COCKTAIL
226

BULMER'S POMAGNE CUP
226

CAPER SAUCE
120

CHEESE SAUCE
121

CHRISTMAS PUDDING
171

CIDER CUP
225

COCONUT CAKES
36

CORNISH PASTY
75

CORNISH SPLITS
49

COTTAGE OR SHEPHERD'S PIE
76

CRUMPETS
35

CUSTARD SAUCE
122

DAMSON CHEESE
158

JERUSALEM ARTICHOKES, BOILED
134

JERUSALEM ARTICHOKES, CHIPS
134

JERUSALEM ARTICHOKE SOUP
134

JUGGED HARE
102

LANCASHIRE HOT POT
74

LEICESTERSHIRE BOSWORTH JUMBELS
48

LEMON CURD OR CHEESE
159

LUNCH CAKE
37

MADEIRA CAKE
38

MAIDS OF HONOR
48

MARMALADE
20

MAYONNAISE SAUCE
122

MINCE PIES
172

MINT SAUCE
118

MONTPELIER BUTTER
178

MUSHROOM PICKLE
137

MUSTARD PICKLE
136

OLD HEREFORDSHIRE CIDER CAKE
225

ONION PICKLE
135

SALAD DRESSING
121

SANDWICH CAKE
40

SAUSAGE MEAT
90

SCONES
35

SCOTCH WOODCOCK
176

SEED CAKE
40

SHEPHERD'S OR COTTAGE PIE
76

SHORTBREAD
52

SHREWSBURY CAKES
50

SHRIMP PASTE OR POTTED SHRIMPS
177

SODA OR IRISH BREAD
190

STUFFED VEGETABLE MARROW
135

SUET PUDDING—ROLY POLYS
174

SUMMER PUDDING
157

VEAL STUFFING
191

WALNUT PICKLE
136

WELSH RAREBIT
176

WHITE FOUNDATION SAUCE
118

YORKSHIRE PUDDING
174